MAX BYGRAVES

STARS
IN MY EYES

A LIFE IN SHOW BUSINESS

ROBSON BOOKS

This paperback edition first published in Great Britain
in 2003 by Robson Books
The Chrysalis Building, Bramley Road, London W10 6SP

An imprint of **Chrysalis** Books Group plc

British Library Cataloguing in Publication Data
A catalogue record for this title is available from the
British Library.

ISBN 1 86105 672 9

Typeset by SX Composing DTP, Rayleigh, Essex
Printed by Creative Print & Design (Wales),
Ebbw Vale

*I would like to dedicate this book
to Blossom and my family . . .*

CONTENTS

AND A STAR SHONE IN THE ☆ EAST . . . END

It was 1950, I was 28 years old and I was in Hollywood. I had been invited by famous American comedian Jack Benny and his wife Mary to their house in Beverly Hills for dinner. When I arrived and sat down to eat, I shared the table with seven guests – famous film stars Ronald Colman and the Marx brother Groucho, Broadway star Ethel Merman, and George Burns with his wife Gracie Allen, people I had only ever seen on the silver screen at a local cinema in Bermondsey as a youngster.

On this evening I sat in awe, wondering how I had been asked to take a chair among some of the entertainment world's biggest star names. It was the first of many invites to similar star-studded evenings. Now in my eightieth year, I can reflect on so many wonderful moments like this, of friends and incidents that are indelible in my memory.

In these following pages I would like to share my personal memories with you, moments that have truly left me with 'stars in my eyes'. From the twenties to my working show business life in the new millennium, it all seems to have happened in a 'twinkling'. With the help of some very helpful help I have been able to remember quite a lot, with the gentle prompting of my son Anthony – some 'don't forgets' from my wife Blossom, plus drawers full of photographs, I am able to jog my memory with a few vivid reminders.

I would also like to say a special thank you to Chris Woodward for use of his London Palladium Collection and for supplying historical background information, Doug Mackenzie for archive photographic material, the Robert Opie Collection for billboard posters, Universal Pictorial Press & Agency Ltd. for use of the photograph of the Beverley sisters, to my son Anthony and his wife Celia for typing and helping to assemble the manuscript and photographic material, to my editors, Norma Macmillan and Alison Leach, Jeremy Robson, Jane Donovan, Sharon Benjamin, Richard Mason and Bob Crocker at Robson Books; also to my family, friends and many show business colleagues, without whom this book and its varied content would not have been possible and to God for giving me the health and strength to still be working.

There is no spite or 'clever dick' thinking in these pages – I find it hard to be cruel to old friends, so if you're looking for sensation, close the book. This is a little chat between you and me. Please enjoy.

Max Bygraves OBE
London, 2002

OVERTURE AND BEGINNERS

Rotherhithe is on that bend in the River Thames seen nightly on BBC's *Eastenders*. If you happened to live near that bend in the thirties, as we did, you'd have noticed several times a month a body being washed up, then being taken to the mortuary, which was about a hundred yards away in St Marychurch Street. These were mostly suicides, people who either couldn't stand the hardships or lovers who'd decided to end it all. Or it could be they were able-bodied lightermen who might have had a drop too much and missed their footing steering a barge down river. Whatever, these and other flotsam were washed ashore at Rotherhithe because the current went that way.

For the early part of my life, this was my playground. If I were to write about the poverty and our struggle for survival, you'd think I was stealing pages from that wonderful chronicle on a dog's life entitled *Angela's Ashes*. There were parts of that book I could identify with – the food shortage, the sharing of beds, and all six of us kids (me, my brother and four sisters) also sharing measles because our parents couldn't quarantine us in our one-bedroom council flat. The hand-me-downs were never handed down because we wore them till they were threadbare.

Hey! Don't get me wrong. I had a wonderful childhood, a good mother who was gentle, kind, loving, shy and generous, and a father who brought us up with a code of honour. He tried hard to make himself worthy. The trouble was we were poor and when you are poor, with a family of eight to provide for, living in a two-room flat and with no wages because of unemployment . . . Well, you are poor. There's no other word for it. That's why I don't want to dwell on those days. I'd rather go on to my fourteenth year, when I left school and became a wage-earner. That's when I feel I began to 'live', and the time when I gave thanks to a fellow named 'Hitler'.

Dear Adolf. He was responsible for the demolition of many a house and flat that the council had 'condemned', but did little or nothing about. He was also responsible for my brother Harry, my younger sister and me getting into uniform – all in the RAF – and being issued with warm suits, good footwear and three square meals daily, plus a regular wage, measly but regular. Thanks, Adolf. We escaped unscathed . . .

But that's jumping the gun at this stage, so let's go back to my fourteenth year, when I had left school with a certificate. It was only for swimming the hundred-yard freestyle, but it was the first time I'd had my name written on any accomplishment: 'Walter William Bygraves'. It made me so proud and I treasured it . . . until my father needed a piece of paper to write a bet out for the local bookmaker and tore a large piece off the left-hand corner. It was a winning bet, but he heard me sobbing and so asked Sid Read, the bookmaker, if he could have the original bet back. He bought a roll of sticky tape to repair the certificate,

STARS IN MY EYES ☆

which remained dog-eared until it finished up in a Second World War salvage pack.

Thinking of those childhood days, I can never remember being bored. I lived every minute of every hour, every day. Later on in life one of my compositions was for a song that became the title for a CD: *Back in My Childhood Days*. It was most successful and gave me a great deal of financial pleasure. The lyrics may stir a few memories for the reader.

Back in my Childhood Days
Words and Music by Max Bygraves

The things that we did when I was a kid
Keep coming back to me
The games that we played and the friends that we made
Keep haunting my memory
I'm full of nostalgia remembering when
The biff-bat and the yo-yo were the craze
Garbo and Myrna Loy
Jolson and Sonny Boy
Back in my childhood days

Uncle George wore a monocle
We read the News Chronicle
Back in my childhood days
There was Gandhi and Lenin
Lady Astor and Bevin
Back in my childhood days
We all used to cram on a 68 tram
The railways didn't have those long delays
The gentry played polo
Amy Johnson flew solo
Back in my childhood days

Ten fags cost fourpence
A pint cost the same

Back in my childhood days
Rhubarb and custard
Corned beef and mustard
Back in my childhood days
I once saw a Zeppelin up in the sky
I saw the Crystal Palace all ablaze
We joined the Boy Scouts or we grew up as louts
Back in my childhood days

We all used to sing
Songs recorded by Bing
Back in my childhood days
There were carousel rides
We had short back and sides
Back in my childhood days
Fishing with worms
All the ladies had perms
They didn't wear a bra, they called 'em 'stays'
There was Popeye the sailor
And the fifty-bob tailor
Back in my childhood days

If we ever got sick
We were rubbed in with Vick
Back in my childhood days
If any spots were seen
Straight into quarantine
Back in my childhood days
Friday night was bath night
With syrup of figs
You'd spit it out all over the place
And the Doctor would come if you'd a rash on your bum
Back in my childhood days

It's amazing the letters I get from interested people familiar with names and places identified in that particular song. Names like Amy Johnson, Lobby Lud and others around in the thirties. It's understandable. My father often spoke of a corrupt politician named Horatio Bottomley who went to gaol for 'fiddling'. Dad, being an honest ex-pugilist who fought by the rules, had no time for dishonesty, and offered this name Bottomley to my brother and me as a type to avoid when we grew up and went out into the big wide world.

The big wide world for me at fourteen was an advertising agency, W S Crawford, at 233 High Holborn. The address was more awesome than anything in Rotherhithe. High Holborn was the location of the Prudential Assurance Company and several other giants, including Pearl Insurance and Gamages, a large department store that supplied most goods, including bicycles. I later purchased one of these there to save my shoe leather while 'hoofing it', delivering copy to Fleet Street for Crawford's.

In Rotherhithe, the nearest I could get to a taxi ride was a number 13 bus to London Bridge on the way home at night. The chances of meeting a famous celebrity were as remote as Joan Collins becoming Pope. I met Joan and became friendly with her years later . . . But back to the thirties.

I had become aware of somebody named 'Bill Stickers'. In most lavatories and on fences there was invariably a notice saying 'Bill Stickers will be Prosecuted'. I swear that for a long time I honestly believed 'Bill' was on the run and that he should have been caught with so many ads requesting his capture. It took a while for my innocent brain to work out that 'Bill Posters' was also wanted and that he and 'Bill Stickers' were one and the same man.

Posters on hoardings were a joy to behold. The best was when a poster had gone past its sell-by date. Then a new one would be pasted up by a bill sticker on some busy thoroughfare. The 'Bisto Kids' was one campaign that changed ads frequently. I don't profess to be John Betjeman, but several publications liked my piece on 'Bill Stickers' and took it for their pages. Here it is.

Bill Stickers

D'ye remember those placards and posters
They posted on hoardings up high
Remember the man with the bucket and paste
And a ladder that reached to the sky?

He'd take out a poster some twelve feet by six
Then cover the back part with glue
And there it would stay – for a year and a day
As the world down below stopped to view.

He pasted up posters for Bovril
R White's advertised ginger beer
Wincarnis was wine that made you feel fine
Especially if you were queer.

There was young Denis Compton for Brylcreem
And glacier mints made by Fox;
And one I remember said, 'Take Beecham's Pills -
They're worth a guinea a box!'

Jacob's Cream Crackers, Libby's Tinned Milk
And biscuits made by Peek Freans;
They advertised Eno's to get rid of wind
Right next to an ad for baked beans.

Horlicks is one that stays in my mind
'Horlicks will stop night starvation'.
And little square chocolates called Ex Lax
For people that had constipation.

One ad that made the unemployed smile
They thought it such a big joke
'For only six hundred – own a Rolls Royce!'
Most of the poor sods were broke.

There were posters for weekends in Paris
And seaside resorts down in Kent.
There was one that simply said – Durex
I was too young to know what that meant.

But now they've all vanished – Bill Stickers is dead,
His ladders and paste you don't see
He's gone, like the man with the pole that lit lamps
And for this you can thank ITV.

The top advertising poster of the day was for petrol. It featured speed ace Sir Malcolm Campbell, the fastest man on earth, who had broken the land-speed record at no less than 150.766 mph in 'Bluebird' at Pendine Sands. His son Donald was to die on Lake Coniston on 4 January 1967 while trying to break his own water-speed record. I once heard Donald telling my son that one of the hardest things in his life was having to live up to his father's achievements. It's tough to have to follow in a father's footsteps – I'm glad I didn't have to follow my dad in the boxing ring . . .

At Crawford's, I was a messenger boy, turning up every day in collar and tie, with shoes polished and hair brilliantined. We messengers were under the watchful eye of Mrs Zelinskey, a 50-year-old widow who constantly passed through the despatch department, stopping to tell us to 'Sit up straight'. We had to bring her a cup of tea from the kitchen at 3 p.m. sharp and it had to arrive hot. One of our team, whose surname I remember being Barnes, had the tea-delivery job one day and was so nervous of Miss Zelinskey's forbidding gaze that he arrived at her desk with half the hot tea in the saucer. He was never chosen as tea carrier again.

From that day on, we all referred to him as Nippy, the name given to the waitresses at Lyons Corner Houses.

One sunny afternoon, I was told to go to the office of the boss, Sir William Crawford, to collect a letter for delivery. After I knocked at the door a loud voice shouted, 'Come in!' I entered the elaborate modern Art Deco office, designed by artist Ashley Havinden (he did most of the macho ads for Simpson's of Piccadilly, including the Daks and Simpson menswear ads). Sitting at the desk, which was almost as big as the flat I lived in at Rotherhithe, was Sir William Crawford, a dead ringer for film star Sydney Greenstreet. He chose his words carefully, as if talking to an idiot. Holding the letter between thumb and finger, he asked, 'And your name is?'

'Bygraves, Sir William,'

'Ah – Sir William Bygraves.'

'No, sir. Wally.'

'Oh, Wally Bygraves.'

'Yes, sir.'

'Well, Wally, I would like you to go downstairs, hail a taxi and then give the driver instructions to take you to Fortnum and Mason's in Piccadilly.'

'Yes, sir.'

'When you arrive at Fortnum's take about ten steps back towards Piccadilly Circus. Are you still with me?'

'Yes, sir.'

'Look at the numbers on the door [he wrote the number on a memo]. Then at this one – this number – ring the bell. Who will answer the door?'

'I don't know, sir.'

'Have you heard of Sir Malcolm Campbell?'

'Yes, sir,' I blinked.

'Hand this very important letter to him.'

'How do I pay for the taxi, sir?'

'Here.' Sir William passed me two half crowns, adding, '. . . and give a threepenny tip to the driver.'

After paying the driver the exact fare and figuring I needed the tip more than he did, I pushed the bell at the given number on Piccadilly. A short wait and then, expecting a maid or valet to appear, the door opened to reveal the bronzed smiling man of the moment, Sir Malcolm Campbell, somebody I had only seen on a poster advertising Shell petrol. He mumbled something in a foreign tongue, which I later discovered was a Scottish accent. To this day I don't know what he said. I understood though when he fished in his waistcoat pocket for sixpence and gave me the coin with 'Here y'are, laddie' and a big kindly smile, then gently closed the door.

With what I had made from Sir William's taxi ride plus Sir Malcolm's tip, I felt super rich. Walking into Fortnum's food counter I bought two custard tarts and got threepence in change. Wow! Big money! I made my way to the small church a few doors away and ate like a navvy, both tarts in one gulp, without spilling the custard.

That evening I couldn't wait to get home to tell my mates of my meeting with speed ace Sir Malcolm Campbell. But my story was 'topped' by mate Willie Perkins who could shoot a line better than I could. On that very same day, he had opened a taxi door in the Strand for Hollywood star Errol Flynn, who had tipped him a shilling.

While working as a messenger boy at Crawford's, I became more and more interested in poster design. So much so that I disliked being sent out on jobs that entailed lugging heavy leaded blocks to the Fleet Street area, delivering them to newspapers – the *Daily Express*, *Daily Telegraph* and *Daily Mail* at Northcliffe House. I also delivered them to weeklies like *Punch* at Bouverie House, but I liked that particular call because there was a pretty girl at the reception. After she had signed my delivery book she gave me that week's copy of *Punch*. Although I didn't always understand the jokes and cartoons, I began to appreciate who they were aimed at.

The reason I disliked being away from Crawford's for more than an hour or so was I had a pal there, Mr Pierce, who was giving me an insight into copy writing, printing block proofs and lots of other things I knew nothing about. I wanted to better myself – the salary increase was a great consideration.

Another reason was just two or three yards from Crawford's main entrance – the popular theatre, the Holborn Empire, where most of the top liners appeared. Until it was bombed by the Luftwaffe, to 'pros' the Empire was a more important date than the London Palladium (at that time the Palladium was what they call 'a white elephant'). The Holborn Empire was the place that set my pulses racing.

The programme was changed weekly, as were the black and white 8×10 photographs in the glass frames outside. A regular performer was the popular Max Miller. I once saw him arrive in a taxi at the stage door. I stood looking at him in awe, never dreaming that one day we'd be sharing the same stage, or that we'd appear on a Command Performance together. And that I would be on a TV programme called *This is Your Life*, with Max saying nice things about me. But more about that later . . . I can still remember standing outside the stage door of the Holborn, watching the great Max pay the driver and make a dive for the stage door, while giving me a friendly wink of his eye. That moment has stayed with me for ever.

I could just afford a seat in the gallery at the Holborn. In those days it cost a shilling (5p). From way up there, a long distance from the stage, the performers looked tiny. In fact, once when Wee Georgie Wood walked on stage I thought I'd gone blind.

At that time, when microphones were unreliable, it was the performers who were 'verbal' who could always be heard anywhere in the theatre. The expert at voice projection was Max Miller. He made sure everybody heard him. It was part of his enormous popularity. One line I remember him delivering was: "ere! There's a lady down there with a hearing aid. 'ello, love, you won't need that. I say, you won't need that, lady. I thought so – she's switched it off!'

Harmless repartee. Max just made something out of any situation. If, like me, your dreams were of going into show business, you couldn't have had a better teacher. Nobody did it better. All these thoughts were a long way off, though, and would not actually materialise until Adolf Hitler came passing by. Thanks again, Adolf.

THE WAR

The newspapers, the radio and general conversation were talking of little else but the situation in Europe. Hitler's army appeared to be walking around as if they owned the place, and were causing the most horrific suffering (none of us knew just how horrific those sufferings were until after the war had ended). Mr Chamberlain went to Munich for a word with Herr Hitler and came back with that famous piece of paper, which said that we were going to continue to enjoy 'peace'. Optimism made us want to believe him, but when we saw more and more gas masks being made in our factories, and the German Army moving ever closer to Poland, a country Britain had vowed to defend, our more practical side knew that there was bound to be trouble ahead.

On 3 September 1939, at 11 a.m., everyone gathered around their radios to hear Mr Chamberlain broadcast to the nation. We were at war with Germany! It is difficult to describe exactly what it meant to us. Everybody knew that it was grave news, but, at the same time, there was an instant demonstration of the sort of spirit that the British people keep stored up for just such an occasion – a mixture of fear, determination, anger and resolve. This was coupled with the belief that the situation would only last six months at the most.

In one way or another, the entire nation was affected by the news. My brother Harry enlisted immediately and joined the Royal Engineers. After some heavy training he went off to France to fight. I was still only seventeen and so under the age for recruitment, much to my mother's relief. My dad continued working as a docker. Because the government designated this as a specialised trade, dockers could be moved about the country to wherever the need was greatest. So during the war years he went to Liverpool, Cardiff and Glasgow, as well as working in London.

I lost my job. I hadn't done anything wrong, but Crawford's, like many other advertising agencies, went out of business – soon after hostilities were announced, newspapers were cut down to single broadsheets and there was no longer the advertising space to fill. So I went to Paddock Wood in Kent for three weeks and earned a bit of cash by hop-picking. It was good fun, a healthy occupation, and you got paid for it. Whitbread's owned the farm and we were looked after. Unfortunately, when the harvest was over we all had to 'hop it' back to London.

Because I could make pipe-racks and pastry-boards I became a carpenter's apprentice and worked in the building trade for a company called F G Minter. They paid me twice as much as I had been earning at Crawford's, which was pretty useful since we no longer had the contribution from Harry. One of my first jobs was helping to put up air-raid shelters at Crosse and Blackwell's soup factory in Bermondsey. So, if anyone remembers taking refuge in those shelters, yours truly had a hand in them.

I was only an apprentice, of course, and since air-raid shelters did not require pipe-racks or pastry-boards, there was a limit to the expression of my obvious talents. The experienced carpenters took me under their wing and gave me the opportunity to do what I was really good at: I swept up, sharpened their chisels and made sure that there was always a bucket of tea on the go. Yes, a *bucket* of tea! We thought 'hygiene' was something you would shout in greeting to a girl named Jean!

The tea was obtained from a local café . . . until I came to an arrangement with an aunt of mine, who lived nearby. Between us we made a small profit, not much, but enough to make it worth doing. The deal ended when we moved to another area to work, but it was a lucrative enterprise while it lasted.

I was more than a little keen to join up but I was still not old enough, so I continued with my job. I became quite friendly with a carpenter by the name of Albert. He was heavily into entertainment and used to give charity performances with a little concert party that he had brought together. Albert did some comedy routines, and there was music from another bloke who was a baritone, two female singers and an accordion player. They all did their own spots but also combined it with comedy patter, and usually finished their show by all taking part in a well-known routine called 'If I Were Not Upon The Stage . . .'

When Albert heard me singing and doing impressions at work he invited me to join the concert party. So, for a while, I went around with them after work visiting air-raid shelters and taking part in the show. Some nights the bombing was too severe to go home and we stayed in the shelter. Everyone mucked in. We did not get paid to entertain, but being able to share in the tea and sandwiches and to take everyone's minds off the horrors of war was reward enough.

Some nights the bombing did not start until after we had left the shelter and were on our way home. I prayed a good many times when I was on my own and heard the drone of German aircraft, which heralded the thudding and crashing of bombs. At Rotherhithe we were an easy target because of the bend in the river, and the dense area of homes and industry. The enemy pilots did not have to think about any particular target, the whole of Rotherhithe would do. I have never known anything so frightening in my life, and I still cringe whenever I think about it. I'm sure that all of us who have experienced something like that can never forget it.

The concert parties were good fun. I mostly did my impersonations and joined the others in the Finale routine. One of my best impersonations was of Arthur Tracy, who used to be billed as the 'Street Singer'. He was well known for singing a song called 'Marta'. My impersonation of him used to go down really well and I found it worked best if I saved Arthur until the end. I was learning the lesson of how to organise your act. Another of my more popular impersonations was Max Miller. I used to spend ten minutes doing him. I knew his routine by heart and did an exact repeat of him and his material. It went very well indeed. The foundations were being put down for young Walter Bygraves to build himself a career in show business.

The bomb damage in London meant that it was 'all hands on deck' for carpenters to repair things as much, and as quickly, as possible. Even I was given hammer and nails and told to do my best. By the time I had finished, there were a number of homes all over South London that looked remarkably like pipe-racks.

One day I was on a roof, fixing a joist that had been damaged by a bomb blast the night before. It was morning, so when the air-raid siren went off, I didn't take it too seriously, thinking that Adolf did the opposite of Red Indians and attacked only at night! When I looked up into the sky and saw the unmistakable outline of several German bombers, I began to take it all a lot more seriously.

No more than a hundred yards away a bomb struck. The tremor shook the roof on which I was working and I slid down the tiles to the gutter. I grabbed the top of my ladder with one hand, to stop myself diving a straight thirty feet on to the concrete below. The ladder held firm for a split second and then began to topple, taking me with it. As it crashed to the ground, it catapulted me into a large privet hedge, which was altogether a better choice than the pavement, but still had the same effect as wrestling with a porcupine.

The woman who owned the house hurried up to me, looked down at my crumpled position in her privet and adopted the classic pose of hand on hip. Wagging her finger at me, she nagged, 'You should have been down the shelter!'

I didn't know what to say . . . or rather, I knew what I wanted to say, but, after all, I had been brought up a gentleman!

I decided to take a lunch break and went to the local café. As I gazed out of the window I kept seeing buses go past with 'Yorkshire Grey' emblazoned on them. It sounds like a kind of tea, but in fact it was the name of a well-known pub in Eltham. It had become even more well known as the centre for medical examinations for volunteers to the armed forces. My experience on the roof had shown me that it was quite possible to get killed in wartime, without even trying, so my resolve to do something constructive became even stronger.

I finished my tea and jumped on the next bus to the 'Yorkshire Grey'. I passed the medical exam in A1 condition and three days later got my papers to report to RAF Cardington. I didn't have the heart to tell my mother, so I left a note on the mantelpiece addressed to both my parents, telling them what I had done and assuring them that I loved them all and would take good care of myself. Much later, I was told that my mother had a good cry and then she hiccupped back the tears and said: 'What is he doing in the RAF? He can't even drive a plane!' Mums are wonderful, aren't they?

Although the country had been full of men and women who wanted to rid themselves of this enemy, and seemed to make light of it all, suddenly things became serious. This Adolf started sending big aeroplanes over our little island, and these planes carried bombs and began dropping them all over the place. My Charlie Chaplin impersonation wasn't funny anymore. Something had to be done – and I did it. I joined the RAF. After all, it would all be over in a couple of weeks.

Although I had been passed A1, there was a slight problem with my eyesight, and that stopped me from joining air crew. Instead I joined the team of fitters on air-frames. My first evening in the RAF was to be something that I would never forget. How could I? It changed my entire life!

Not yet having been issued with uniforms we were still in civvies when we were ushered into the NAAFI for our first evening in the forces. My attention was drawn to a pianist who was struggling through a rendition of 'In the Mood'. He wasn't so much tinkling the ivories as torturing them. I'm sure that if Glenn Miller had come in then, he would have shot himself. A sergeant walked on to the stage and addressed us. Behind his benign smile, there was obviously a malignant spirit of sadism, but he hid it well. He told us what to expect from our first full day in the RAF, what we would be issued with, what life in future was going to be like, and just about everything else that we needed to know but would probably forget before too much time had passed.

My ears pricked up when he told us that we would have to provide our own entertainment. Entertainment! Did somebody mention entertainment? He asked if any of us had been entertainers before the war started. One chap put up his hand and explained that he had been singing with the D'Oyly Carte Opera Company. He was called on to the stage and gave us a rendering of 'Bless This House', which was really very good. Nobody doubted that he was a pro.

When the sergeant asked if there was anyone else who

had done any entertaining, I put up my hand and said I could do an impersonation of Max Miller. Next thing I knew I was on the stage doing the Max Miller routine that I had performed back in Rotherhithe. It went very well, and I was given a lot of applause and back-slapping as I returned to my seat. Several of the lads assumed that I was a professional. I have to admit it made me glow with pride a little bit, especially when I thought back to all those stars I'd seen at the Holborn Empire and realised that I was being put in the same category with them.

From that moment on, everyone called me Max, and that is what I have been called ever since. That's why that first evening at RAF Cardington was so significant – it was the birth of Max Bygraves!

I was also Bygraves, Aircraftsman Second Class, number 1212094. Not long after arriving at Cardington, we were all sent for our initial square-bashing in Bridgnorth, that lovely town on the Shropshire border. To me it was the lap of luxury because I had my own bed, good food and a host of instant mates. I also had a most uncomfortable experience.

I was given an evening pass, which meant that I could go out into town for some entertainment, returning in a lorry provided for the purpose of bringing us all back at midnight. I made off on my own to have a look around the town, dutifully carrying my gas-mask, an immediate clue to other more experienced servicemen that I was a rookie. I didn't fancy the entertainment that was on offer, because the cinema was closed and the pubs were all short of beer. The YMCA was not really my cup of tea so, after wandering around for a while, I decided to walk back to camp rather than wait the hours for the truck.

It was approaching dark when I left the town. I faced a walk of a couple of miles, which was not a problem because I was well used to 'shanks's pony'. Seeing the camp lights in the distance, I suddenly had a brainstorm and decided that it would be much more sensible to cut across the fields than to follow the winding road. As I walked across one field all the lights in the camp suddenly went off – the black-out of course! I was forced to follow my nose. As I climbed the fence and ventured into the next field I gradually became aware of a presence. I didn't know what it was but there was definitely something else in the field. I froze!

Whatever it was came closer, and then suddenly the whole field turned into bedlam – I was in the midst of hundreds of chickens, shrieking and squawking at the tops of their voices, taking off in all directions! Needless to say, I took off as well. They must have been pretty stupid chickens, though. I mean, do I look like a fox? Anyway, in my rush to get out of there, I dived through a barbed-wire fence, which made my hands, face and uniform look like shredded wheat. I ran all the way back to camp and slipped into bed as quietly as possible.

Next morning I was in absolute panic. How could I appear on parade in my condition and with my uniform in tatters? I tried to think of all the different ways round the problem, but, in the end, the inevitable happened. I stood there being looked at, up and down, by the man in charge, Flight Sergeant English, who was actually a Welshman. He demanded an explanation, in no uncertain terms, and, after stammering and stuttering, I eventually came clean.

I began hesitantly to tell my sorrowful tale about the previous night's events, but was interrupted by one of my new mates, Ben Slennet, who could sweet-talk a turkey into walking into an oven.

'Excuse me sir, but he's not telling the truth!' Ben went on to spin this yarn about how I had been accosted by six soldiers and had taken exception to the way they insulted the RAF. By the time he had finished, I was a hero, and Flight Sergeant English was beaming at me. I was sent for medical treatment and a new uniform. All was forgiven, just so long as I was defending the honour of his beloved RAF. Ben and I have met up quite a lot since then and always have a laugh about the incident. I hope Flight Sergeant English did, too, when he eventually found out the truth.

Just as a little diversion, if anyone reading this believes that they may have served with me in the RAF during that time, they have a fifty-fifty chance of being correct. You see, there were two Walter William Bygraves knocking about, and we share the same birth date. In fact, we share the same birth certificate and the same mum and dad. Allow me to explain.

I mentioned that my brother Harry had joined the Royal Engineers and gone to France. Well, he was among those who were evacuated from the beaches of Dunkirk and, when he arrived back in Britain, he didn't report to his unit. He came straight home, totally exhausted, and slept for a solid three days. When he started to get back into the land of the living, he realised that he could not face another Dunkirk, so he 'borrowed' my name and birth certificate and joined the RAF. All the details were the same except that we had different numbers.

My mother received a letter saying that Harry was among those unaccounted for at Dunkirk and was told that the War Office would be in touch again when they had more news. She never heard any more. My father's sense of humour came to the fore, when he heard that his two sons were now both in the RAF under the same name and initials. 'Wouldn't be funny if one of you got shot and they buried the other one!' he said.

Thanks, dad!

Friendships that develop in the Forces are never forgotten. I have already mentioned Ben Slennet, but there was also Jimmy Cairns, a Scots lad from Greenock who had a problem with his adenoids and could not stop sniffing. One day the drill sergeant shouted at him: 'Haven't you got a handkerchief, Cairns?'

Quick as a flash, Jimmy replied: 'Yes, sir, but I don't lend it to strangers!' Jimmy was sent to the cookhouse to do washing-up duty, and yours truly went with him for laughing at the quip. Jimmy and I became inseparable.

Another pal was Harry Woods. We all knocked about together and went from Bridgnorth to Weston-super-Mare for a crash course – no pun intended – on being fitters, before being transferred to Hornchurch in Essex, a lot closer to home for me. Harry decided to get married and asked me to be his best man. I was delighted, and we got our passes sorted out for the trip to Liverpool where the lucky lady and Harry were to be wed.

Liverpool was like a foreign country to me – Bridgnorth had been the farthest north that I had ever travelled. I was unprepared for the Liverpudlian hospitality and a wedding reception that went on for several days. When we finally arrived back at the RAF camp on the Tuesday night, we were well past our weekend pass deadline. So inevitably we were in all sorts of trouble and were given fourteen days' detention, which meant a lot of running in full pack, loss of privileges, a solitary cell and loss of pay. It turned out to be an expensive weekend, but a lot of fun.

Ben Slennet became my agent in a way. I was just turning eighteen and Ben was twice my age. He seemed to be dedicated to getting himself out of the RAF at the earliest opportunity, and was excused just about everything that it was in his interests to be excused from. As I said before, he could charm the spikes off a cactus. In best 'Bilko' fashion he arranged all sorts of jobs for himself, and always enlisted me as his assistant. He could make a half-hour lino-polishing job last all day, and taught me the ropes, with a crash course – yes, another one – on 'malingering'. Ben was a master. But don't think that he was lazy, he wasn't. When he wanted to work, he could work well, and work fast, but he didn't believe in allowing life to push him around. Nowadays he would be referred to as a 'control freak'.

Having become his 'protégé' in the art of malingering, I then became his 'show business' client, and he started to get me appearances at social functions. I can remember him arranging for me to do my stuff at a Buffaloes' do. That reminds me of the kid who came home from school with some homework about animals and asked his dad, 'How do buffaloes make love?' His dad shrugged, and said, 'It's no good asking me, lad, I'm a Freemason!'

Anyway, Ben agreed a fee of £1 for me to do this Buffaloes' event, with his agent's fee deducted. It was good pay, much more than I was getting per week with the RAF. The only problem was, how to get an evening pass. Ben saw to that. He went to the Orderly Officer and told him that I was going to do a charity show for the Buffs, with the proceeds going to the Red Cross. We got our passes and the evening was a success. The Buffs enjoyed it so much that they happily paid the fee and gave us a bottle of champagne as well. On the way home we split the fee and the champagne, and arrived back at camp in good spirits. It was the start of a career move for me, as Ben followed that with all kinds of other appearances. I don't know how he fixed half of them, but I was getting paid to enjoy myself, so I wasn't arguing. Not only did Ben keep the dates coming, he never failed to get us the passes. He was a real pro.

Not all the gigs I did were paid ones, but those that were turned out to be pretty good. Whenever there was the chance of a weekend pass, Ben used to contact various pubs and arrange bookings. Even then, I didn't realise that I was being paid to perform and that I was now a professional entertainer. Being a bit dim, I never gave it a second thought, other than the fact that we were getting a few bob on the side for having a bit of fun.

I used to go home and see the family whenever I could. Like most East Londoners, they were in the front line of the bombing raids, and it took its toll, with houses disappearing, together with friends and neighbours. I caught my mother a little the worse for gin one night, and it made me angry that I couldn't get her to come to her senses. I went

Left Voted the best act in the RAF's Fighter Command. Suit by Moss Bros.

Above right Suit and forage cap by HM Government.

Right On honeymoon (1942) – suit, shirt and tie by elder brother Harry.

Left *Do Re Mi*, a tough show – on stage throughout.

Centre On the way to Mike Todd's around the world première – good thing we had a life belt.

Below Two of the sweetest words to an actor… 'House full'.

Look at those names on one bill – all working for free.

Above Another star-studded evening: Command Performance (1953).

Below With some of the cast of *Cry From the Streets* (1958).

Above With Hal Monty in the comedy, *Skimpy in the Army*. When this film crops up on TV, I run and hide.

Below 'Tulips From Amsterdam'.

Below With Pat Driscoll in *Charley Moon* (1956).

Above Dana Wilson in *Cry From the Streets*, doing her impression of Mrs Thatcher.

Right What a knight!

Below Donald Pleasance in *Spare the Rod* (1961) – 'use the knife'.

Left *Spare the Rod* – a good movie.

Centre Sir Larry Olivier and Roger Moore recording 'fairy stories for grown-ups'.

My favourite leading lady – Barbara Murray in *Cry From the Streets*.

Left Judy Garland and self at the Palace – New York, not Buckingham…

Below left Aye, aye!

Below right 'Goldie', a four-legged friend.

off in a huff, but as I travelled back to camp I began to realise how selfish I had been. I was having an easy time in the RAF, but for people like my mum and her friends, the war was far from being a bit of fun. They had to have something to lean on at times.

I silently wept and vowed that I would one day make it up to my mother for my selfishness. She had once held high hopes that I would become a priest. Instead her son was growing into an uncaring specimen who wanted everything to be the way that he wanted it to be. I chastised myself with my own thoughts and decided to sort myself out.

I WAS STATIONED THERE...

As I drive around the country these days I am surprised to see how many RAF camps remain where I was stationed. My son, and sometimes driver, Anthony, chuckles when I remark, 'I was stationed there !' It's true. I was continually on the move, being posted all over Fighter Command. It's where most of the action took place during the early days of the war.

When not on duty I was performing at various RAF functions, and it meant that I was backed by some really good musicians. By now I wasn't just doing impressions, I was also singing popular songs, and that meant getting to know musicians quite well. One of them was Ray Ellington, who became very famous indeed, both in his own right and as a regular on the legendary *Goon Show*. We worked together many times and for many years after, but first came together in the RAF.

Almost every RAF station I was posted to had requests for amateur or professional performers. I couldn't wait to

24

put my name down: 'LAC Max Bygraves (impressionist, singer, comedian)'. I was immediately sent for by the Entertainment Officer, who would ask me to 'do my stuff'. I had a sort of audition worked out, which invariably impressed, and 'Voilà!' I was included in the concert party – and loving it. It was at RAF Uxbridge I met my first flesh and blood celebrity. It was 1943 and his name was Harrison – F/Lt Harrison – who sent for me because he 'needed help'.

He talked ever so posh, seeming to enunciate each word as he peered at me with a squint, weighing me up for a good ten seconds. 'Mmmm – I hope you can help,' he murmured to himself, 'otherwise we'll all be up the creek.' He explained that I had been sent to help set up a concert that would be the finals in a competition to find the best act in Fighter Command. Concerts in various stations had whittled down the two hundred entrants from all the different aerodromes to fourteen performers. At Uxbridge they were to perform for the Hayes Cup, a large silver trophy. F/Lt Harrison had no idea how to plan the running order, so that comedian didn't follow comedian, harmonica players were separated and anybody making bird noises didn't rain on someone else's parade.

I was told that F/Lt Harrison had been an actor in civvy street and was known as Rex. He played mostly West End theatres and even made films. There were two Rex Harrisons – one who portrayed Professor Higgins in *My Fair Lady* and the other who I knew *was* 'Professor Higgins': vague, rude, dithering and a self-confessed idiot. At first it fooled me, but as we got to know each other, I could see he worked on this eccentricity to cover a multitude of faults.

I made up the running order as best I knew how – making sure I wasn't on too early and managing to put myself before the interval. After the show in the officers' mess, when Rex was being congratulated right and left on the wonderful job he had done as producer, he pointed at me saying, 'I couldn't have done it without the help of this little bugger.' I carried on eating my egg sandwich. I was happy too – I'd won the cup!!

Many years later, on a charity bash at the London Coliseum, we shared a dressing room. I reminded Rex of the concert at Uxbridge when we were all in uniform, and I was a LAC and he was a F/Lt. 'What a wonderful night,' I said. Rex, still keeping up his Professor Higgins eccentric role, said, 'Was it a wonderful night? I don't remember, old boy.' He laughed when I said, 'Sod off, Flight Lieutenant.'

Like most young men of nineteen, I had a healthy interest in the opposite sex. I wouldn't say that I was likely to land a part as Casanova, but I knew what it was like to share a bag of chips and a pickled onion in a bus shelter. I suppose my initial chat-up lines lacked a little finesse, but there was a war on. Offering to treat a girl to a choc ice was about as good as I got in trying to make the right impression.

There was one WAAF whom, I remember very well indeed. She used to cycle past at about five every morning. Who needed an alarm clock? Not me. This WAAF was worth staying awake all night for! I used to feel rotten all day if I didn't get a glimpse of her. But how to approach her? She was a class act and I just knew that if I managed to speak to her, my mouth would dry up, my tongue would stick to the roof, and I would sound like an Oriental with a cleft palate. There can be nothing worse than when you have finally summoned up the courage to speak to a girl who you really fancy, and you have blurted out your rehearsed introduction, pathetic though it may be, she says, 'What?'

Luck was on my side though. I sang at a camp concert one night. Hang on a moment, I don't mean a 'camp' concert, the Danny La Rue sort, I mean a concert in the camp . . . The next morning I was hanging around waiting for my dream WAAF to cycle pass when, suddenly, she stopped in front of me and actually spoke to me.

'Hello, you're the fellow who was singing with the band last night, aren't you?'

I gulped and managed to nod. Then she asked me if I would write out the words to one of the songs, 'If I Had My Way'. I said I would, and off she cycled. The next morning I waited and she came past as usual. I gave her the paper with the words of the song and then gritted my teeth and put my head on the block.

'Er, I was wondering . . . D'you think I could take you out one night?' To my absolute astonishment and joy she agreed, and we began to go out together regularly.

During the time that we were going out she was promoted to corporal and then to sergeant. All the lads started calling me 'Crawler' as I was going out with a sergeant. I'll never forget that lovely girl because, you see, I married her.

Yes, it was Blossom. We courted in the only way you could in those days – a quick kiss behind the bike shed, notes of endearment and an intertwining of weekend passes.

She took me home to meet her mother, her only parent. I'd like to say that we hit it off from the start. I'd like to say it but, in all truth, when her mum and I met it was dislike at first sight. I didn't mind her so much, but she didn't rate me at all. She wanted her daughter to get involved with the top brass, not the bloke who did the polishing. She wanted her daughter to have a future of silks and satins, and suspected that I would be more likely to supply khaki and hessian.

I blotted my copybook on our first encounter when I discovered that she was a spiritualist. She asked me if I believed in the spirits and I joked, 'Only out of a bottle.' She didn't think it was at all funny, and Blossom didn't help. She was too tense to laugh, so she smiled with her eyes while her lovely mouth remained frozen. Blossom had three sisters and six brothers and they came from Romford in Essex. I got on quite well with the rest of the family, but Mrs Murray was decidedly unimpressed with me.

Blossom's mum had told her kids that she was distantly related to royalty, but I never did find out if it was true. Most of the people that I knew who claimed a royal connection had a regular spot in the King's Head!

If the lads back at camp had called me 'Crawler' for going out with a sergeant, they would certainly have had a field day if they had seen me with Blossom's mum. I really put the charm on, and continually told her how nice she looked in her new hat and all that stuff, hoping that it was not an old one that had been taken out of mothballs. Very gradually the ice turned to water. Although I don't think that I ever became her favourite person, she did put up with me.

Blossom had worked in the movie business before joining the RAF – she tore tickets at the local Roxy! She was madly in love with James Stewart, so if I wanted to get round her, I used to slip into an impersonation of him. She melted every time. I still do it if I'm in trouble!

One thing led to another and I eventually popped the question. To my utter relief she accepted, and I didn't even have to become James Stewart. We were married on 12 September 1942. We were both nineteen and very much in love. Or rather I was in love with her and she was in love with my impersonation of James Stewart. We have never had a cross word since – I know when to keep my mouth shut!

This year, 2002, we have been married sixty years, our diamond wedding anniversary, and I still make her laugh. Sometimes I say to her, straight-faced, 'I thought that when the war was over, marriage didn't count anymore – I thought we'd all go back to our mothers.' I always get the same answer from Bloss: 'You should be so lucky!'

The war was not getting any better. The six months that everyone had originally expected it to last had long passed, and it was only the British spirit that kept everyone going. They were grim times, but nobody wanted to give in. There were many laughs and lots of special songs and moments that put a fine gloss over the many wounds.

To my dismay, I was posted to Scotland, to a place called Drem, which seemed to be in the middle of nowhere. Bloss stayed behind and we had to communicate by letter. I enjoyed every word that she wrote and, hopefully, my meagre offerings meant something to her too. It was awful being away from her. Every day seemed like a month. I had not been away for very long when she wrote me two of the most marvellous words that I've ever read: 'I'm pregnant.'

CURTAIN UP

The war in Europe was over at last. I had been demobbed with the gift of a grey, double-breasted chalk-line suit and the sum of £85 for my contribution to the war. With baby daughter Christine in tow, no home and no job, the first thing Blossom and I did was to purchase a perambulator. At least, then, we were mobile.

After more than four years with the RAF I found demobilisation a shock, a big shock! I was a civilian now. It was wonderful to be free from some of the restrictions that the services *must* have – back in camp by 10.30 p.m. and up early to attend to the 'bullshine', for example. But gone were regular meals at regular times. Gone too was my weekly laundry parcel that I could send and get back in three days – the RAF had supplied my clothes, which included a working set of overalls, a Sunday best for church parades, and footwear I could change when worn out. Gone were the pay parades for pocket money every two weeks. And gone were the comrades I laughed with, played football with and shared cigarettes with. All this was suddenly gone.

Looking back at that time in bombed-out London, with a

wife, baby and very little in the way of money, I remember that at first I really didn't know what to do. But the solution seemed fairly easy – I'd get a job. I was 24. Off to the labour exchange I toddled. When asked my trade I couldn't say. The only answer I could give was what a couple of million other blokes were saying: 'Ex-serviceman.'

The man at the labour exchange asked, 'What service?' I told him the RAF, where I had been an A/C 1 Rigger, working mostly on Spitfires, and that I was pretty good at artwork. 'How do you feel about clearing bomb damage in London?' he asked, then told me this paid £5.10 a week less stamp and insurance. I said, 'Don't you have anything for brain surgeons?' It wasn't his day for smiling. Not only that, there were twenty other chaps lining up behind me looking for work. 'Next,' he called out impatiently.

I took my green card to the foreman of a demolition firm in East Ham, opposite West Ham in London. He asked when I could start. 'Soon as possible,' I told him. 'Have you got overalls?' he asked. Overalls were on clothes rationing and costly, so I turned up next morning in my RAF blue trousers and a pair of boots that we were allowed to keep from our kit when demobbed. Oh yes, and a shirt. 'Crikey,' I thought, 'I really am a civilian again.'

I was given a heavy wheelbarrow to push and told to fill it up with plaster and damaged wood, then to wheel it to a large fire that was constantly burning (that was how London was ridding itself of the acres of bomb damage – tons of it).

Blossom usually wrapped me a cheese and tomato sandwich for my lunch. Sometimes ladies in the bombed-out streets would boil kettles on makeshift fires and bring cups of tea to us. Tea bags were unheard of then, so their tea invariably had grouts in the bottom of the cup. One of the workmen, Pat, a short tubby Irishman, always read the tea leaves in his mug and often read mine. One day, looking intently at the leaves in the bottom of my cup, he murmured, 'Jesus Christ.' I looked at him and asked, 'Jesus Christ what?' He just shook his head in amazement, and kept shaking it. 'Jesus Christ. You lucky bugger.' From that day, whenever I asked what he saw in my tea leaves, all he would say was, 'You lucky bugger.'

At that time of my life I wasn't feeling all that lucky. Gone were those rehearsals for concert parties at almost every RAF station, and gone was the thrill of winning the cup for being the best act in RAF Fighter Command. I felt a bit like my father when his boxing days were over – all he could do was polish the five silver cups he'd won during the first war. Unfortunately, when things had got bad financially he'd pawned them and then never had enough to redeem them, so now he had nothing to gaze at, and the memories weren't so vivid without the cups. That's how I felt without the concert parties and the music always near at hand.

Perhaps the luck Pat had seen in my tea leaves pertained to my lovely wife and friend, Blossom. She had enormous faith in me, faith I lacked myself. How lucky I was to pick a winner in the lottery of life and love. She is still my greatest plugger.

During my service in the RAF I had learned how to put an act together, and there were always experienced people to put me right about things. For example, a pianist who knew how to jot down music would know how to find a key that suited my voice – I didn't know what was meant when the pianist from the band said 'Try it down half a tone' or 'Try it up in A flat'. But I learned that when I sang what I was taught – an 'arpeggio' – somewhere in that run up the scale was my key. Soon it became quite easy to pitch to an arpeggio. And through the help of musicians like A/C 2 Norrie Paramour I learned that 'tacit' meant to go quiet – or 'schtoom', as Norrie put it.

Furthermore, I was usually the leading laughter-maker in the concert party. And I had done some interesting work, amateur of course, but nevertheless work I could add to my cv, such as several broadcasts from Blackpool called *Aircraftsman Smith Entertains*. Another bit of work was *Middle East Merry-go-round*, a BBC programme recorded for the forces out in that battle zone. I have never yet met anybody who heard one of those shows, but they were prepared as meticulously as any broadcast I would be doing in the near future. That was to come . . . But at present I had no place to show off any skill for being entertaining I had picked up when I was a serviceman.

Then I discovered a pub in Dagenham, near where Blossom and the babe were in rooms I was renting. (Rooms? *A* room, ten shillings a week and use of the cruet.) The pub was called The Merry Fiddlers. If you gave a nod to the piano player you could get up on the small stage and give a song.

I was with my brother-in-law, George. It was early evening and the pub was quiet. George pointed at me behind my back, indicating to the piano player that I'd sing a song. The pianist stopped his playing and announced, 'Here's a young fellow to sing for you.' George gave me a push, and I walked up to the stage. The piano player said, 'What's it gonna be?' I said, *'Begin the Beguine.'* He said, 'What key?' I replied, 'C' (I had learned that from Norrie Paramour). I had also learned 'Give me a four-bar intro', which the piano player 'busked' and a lady playing drums picked up. I sang the song as recorded by Chick Henderson with the Joe Loss Orchestra and received nice applause. The guv'nor bought me a pint of Whitbread's, then asked me if I would do another song. So, with a pint inside me, I wandered back to the stage, picked up the microphone and, instead of going into a song , told the drinkers I would do them a few impersonations.

By now there were quite a lot of the regulars in the bar and all of a sudden I felt quite at home there, doing my act . . . into a Max Miller routine, which I knew by heart from watching the great Max . . . then I slid into one of my favourite impressions, The Ink Spots, who were around at the time . . . and finally mimicked Jimmy Durante for good measure.

My brother-in-law was quite proud of me when I finished, and customers were coming over wanting to buy me a drink. George said, 'That was a good impression of Schnozzle.' Everybody did a Schnozzle impression in those days – even my mother when we were kids. If we told her the soup was too thin or the potatoes needed more salt, she'd slap her thighs in Durante style, exclaiming: 'Everybody wants to get into the act!' I told George about my mother's talent and he said, 'Yeah, but she couldn't do the Ink Spots.'

I went to The Merry Fiddlers many times after that initial performance. At first I was a bit disappointed by the applause – or lack of it (the reason for this was that most customers were standing with a drink in their mitts and it was impossible to clap hands without spilling the precious nectar they were holding). But I discovered a unique way of getting applause. I said if they liked what I was doing to stamp their feet. It worked a treat. Of course, the gov'nor Bill Stiles was not too pleased about fifty or sixty patrons stamping their feet. He said it was unsettling the structure in the cellars below, where the beer barrels were kept. But it was too late, the crowd liked the sound they made with their heavy footwear. He didn't smile when I said, 'I'll ask them to remove their boots before they applaud.'

The days dragged at the building site I was working on. A rule at that time was that if a job was 'rained off' there would be no pay. Sometimes it would rain for two or three days. When it did, there was only half a pay packet at the end of the week.

One day, at midday, it started 'chucking it down'. As it looked set in for the day the gang of us were told to go home. But it was useless going home then. Blossom had got a job as a telephone operator in the exchange at Rainham, and Bloss's sister Evelyn looked after baby Christine in her semi-detached. So, as there would be no one at home I decided to jump on a bus going to Oxford Circus, to see the personal appearance of Hollywood star Mickey Rooney at the Palladium. It was a matinee performance starting at 2.30 p.m. With the ten shillings Bill Stiles had 'bunged' me the night before for entertaining a crowd of Rotarians, I decided to treat myself to a front seat in the Upper Circle. I joined the long queue in the rain. It was to turn out to be one of the luckiest days of my life.

As I stood there with the crowd sheltering under umbrellas I spied my ex-entertainments officer mounting the steps to enter the Palladium. I quickly left the queue to say hello to him. He was pleased to see me and asked me what I was doing. When I told him, he shook his head and asked me why I wasn't round at Aeolian Hall in Bond Street. He informed me that the BBC were holding auditions for ex-servicemen and women for a show to be called *They're Out* – all comers welcomed. So I said goodbye to ex-F/Lt Cecil Landau, and ran through the rain to Aeolian Hall to join the dozen or so wannabes auditioning. I was elated, even though I'd given up a chance of seeing Mickey Rooney.

Hair and clothes dripping, I arrived at Aeolian Hall and sat down next to someone I was going to be friends with for many years to come – Frankie Howerd. We were about the same age, same weight and height, and both had the same dreams of making our way in show business. On this particular day, we were auditioning for a producer named Joy Russell-Smith, who was on the lookout for new talent to be included in a radio show called *Variety Band Box*.

'I was hopeless,' said this gangling youth who was very soon to become one of the great post-war comics. 'All I could think of was ooh aah oh ooh – I couldn't remember a line. I fluffed everything.'

He really was nervous and I couldn't help thinking at the

time that if I ever got in that state, I'd find some other job. But little did he know that those oohs and aahs were to impress the BBC producers so much that in another year Frank was to be a household name.

It was one of those auditions where somebody said, 'Thanks for coming. Leave your name and address and we'll contact you.' You left your name and address, but never expected to hear another word.

We didn't hear anything for almost three months. In the meantime we both got booked for a touring revue, *For the Fun of It*, produced by bandleader Jack Payne, opening in Sheffield on 29 July 1946. I shared a dressing room and digs with Frank up and down the British Isles for the next nine months and got to know him very well. We remained friends for the rest of his life.

Frank had his ups and downs, but always came back, was always able to capture a new breed of audience when he had exhausted another. He became bigger than ever with the part of the Roman slave in television's *Up Pompeii*. He also fancied himself as a clairvoyant, always wanting to read people's hands – pretty accurately too.

I have never been one for fortune-telling, but Frank would insist on giving a reading at least once a week. 'One day you will be a millionaire,' he prophesied. You can imagine my reaction – living in digs that cost £2.50 a week; one suit, and wondering what would happen when the tour was over; no trade; a wife and baby to support. The only help we had was from my wife's sister who let us have a room at her house for five shillings a week. And here's this amateur fortune-teller telling me, 'One day you'll be a millionaire.' All I could say was, 'Frank, I think you've got your wires crossed.'

It was the middle of last year (2001) when I heard he had been poorly. I called him on the phone and asked if he'd like to have lunch. He said he would, and I chose one of the best restaurants in London, just the two of us. We talked mostly nostalgia and I asked if he still read hands. He said he did, took my hand and gazed at my palm for a long time. 'Didn't I tell you that one day you'd be a millionaire?' I nodded. 'Didn't it come true?' I nodded again. He gave my hand back and said, 'Well, in that case, pay the bill!' He made a hasty exit from the restaurant, and that was the last time I saw dear Frank alive.

It was the late forties when he first read my hand and I was making more than the average wage-earner – not much, but enough to afford decent digs for our baby Christine and my wife Blossom. But then a bombshell. Bloss told me she was pregnant once more. Now that wasn't in the planning. Fortunately, I had begun to get dates at real theatres in the provinces.

Anthony was born in 1947, in the coldest spell known in Britain for a hundred years. The day he arrived I was about to finish a week's engagement at the Theatre Royal, York. On the Saturday night, I rushed to the railway station and missed my train by one minute. With my pal Art Christinas, I watched the tail light disappearing down the track. We had a six-hour wait in a waiting room with no heating before the next London train blew in – the coldest and most uncomfortable night I have *ever* experienced, and that includes guard duty at night on RAF aerodromes. Later I was to experience the worst dose of flu. I was in bed for almost a week.

The new baby we named Anthony was a joy. Blossom could not stop chuckling at his cheeky ways. With the baby, four-year-old Christine and me stuffed up with flu, we arrived home at our one-room flat in Woolwich to find no landlady. She had been taken ill and was staying with her son in Dagenham.

The house was cold and damp. Then, almost as if a prayer had been answered, a letter arrived on the Monday morning telling us we had been granted a newly built council house near Romford in Essex. You can imagine the happiness this news brought to our lives. Now we could do anything. 'Come on, Max, let's begin! First I'll become someone.' Oh the stars in my eyes at that moment, big shining twinkling stars.

In those days the bookings were not so plentiful, but there was a 'life saver' for acts to make a few extra shillings. During a show, there was a 'chairman' who used a gavel to call 'order' if the crowd did not pay attention or got restless when an act was performing. On the other hand if the act was a crowd-pleaser the chairman would rap loudly three times, which would bring a cheer from the audience – three loud knocks meant the act had been approved for an encore. If an encore was requested, the performer was awarded a ten-shilling bonus.

At that time I would close my act with an impression of Al Jolson. In 1947 Jolson was the number one vocalist on records because of a Warner Brothers movie, *The Jolson Story*. Forgive me for saying it, but it was a good impersonation I did. In fact, when Jolson died suddenly, the BBC had me impersonate him on a one-hour tribute, accompanied by the Stanley Black Orchestra. But back to the chairman doing the knock-knock-knock with his gavel.

I discovered that if I closed on 'Mammy' à la Jolson, the crowd would demand an encore from Mr Chairman. I'd get called back, and would do a further chorus of 'Carolina in the Morning'. Then I'd take a bow and pretend I was finished. The audience would stamp their approval for another encore. I would often do three encores and make an extra thirty bob – big money!

CAUGHT IN THE ACT

When I entered the band of travelling performers, there were hundreds of digs all over the UK – the Actors' Union published a book with addresses in the main cities as well as landladies in the backwaters who catered on a weekly basis (what pros called 'the number three dates'). Strangely enough, the 'number threes' were usually more comfortable than the digs in Manchester or Leeds or Glasgow.

At that time, we were still on ration books – Hitler had been reported killed in his bunker and the war was supposedly over, but rationing went on for another six years. Many theatres had been bombed and remained mere shells for a long time. Theatre land had suffered, as had ordinary people. But they still wanted entertainment, perhaps more than ever. So if you were a variety act at that time there were plenty of dates to fill. For the next few years that's what I was doing.

As the weeks passed and I got more confident, I used a few minutes in my established and accepted act to experiment with new ideas. I could do this because touring the number threes was much more relaxed than the formality of Moss Empires. There they would question every new sentence you uttered. There was little room for argument when the touring manager, Bill Lyon-Shaw, told you that the original script of your act, which had been passed by the Lord Chamberlain's office, must be adhered to. There must be no ad libbing – no matter how big the laugh; there must be no deviation from the script. This is the reason we welcomed those smaller dates – we did not have to answer to the LCO and we could experiment. If it turned out right and a new routine was born, it was the most satisfying moment you could dream of. If it wasn't right you'd toss it out and work on something else. This is what most of us 'new boys' – Benny Hill, Jimmy Edwards, Frankie Howerd, Tommy Cooper and all – were doing all the time.

To be near Blossom and the babes I took engagements playing the nightclubs in London's West End. If that sounds glamorous it shouldn't. Most of the clubs were upholstered sewers and catered for the dregs of London's night life – the toughest audiences an act could experience. We really earned the standard £15 per week they paid us. But in truth we were young and loved every minute of it.

On one particular engagement I 'doubled' with Tommy Cooper. Doubling meant playing two nightclubs in the same evening. At one club, The Blue Lagoon, we'd begin the cabaret at midnight, then rush to the Panama Club about half a mile away and perform to a different crowd about 1 a.m.

It was simple for me to put a raincoat over my dinner suit and run the distance to the second date, but of course much more difficult for Tommy, who not only had to carry two suitcases filled with his tricks but also had to 'load', which means he had to prepare the tricks. This took time. So Tommy would precede me at the first club and follow me at the second. That way he got extra time to get his act ready.

One night, at the second club, the irate boss asked if I'd seen Tommy. I knew he had left The Blue Lagoon well before me, but there was no sign of him. The boss told me to do extra, so I filled in until I saw the huge shape of Tommy enter and make for the dressing room (which was the gents' lavatory). When I could see he was ready I wound up my stint and introduced 'The Great Thomas Cooper'.

If you think his tricks went wrong as a top of the bill, you should have been at the Panama that night. Disaster. I honestly think that was the night he decided to make a living from his tricks misfiring, with the nervous giggle that became an integral part of his repertoire.

When I asked him afterwards what had made him so late, he told me the 'story'. This is how Tommy told it:

'I came out of the club and was walking quickly past Garrards the Jewellers in Regent Street. A policeman stepped out of a doorway to ask me what I had in the two cases. I said, "Magic." He said, "Open the cases." I tried to explain that I did a magic act and that all my tricks were in the cases, but he insisted.

'Course, when I opened the cases all the vases and rings were sparkling under the lights, so he became suspicious. He thought I was a burglar who'd just done a job. At that moment another copper strolled up. He happened to be an amateur conjuror, so to prove I was legitimate he made me perform one of the tricks. So there I was in the middle of Regent Street at half past midnight doing bottle, glass, glass, bottle, glass, bottle . . .'

He then said, 'Max, I've had a frustrating day. Let's get p. . ..d!' So we did.

This was an interesting billboard (see colour plate) – advertising a bill I wasn't featured on. Indeed, I was appearing at the Finsbury Park Empire a couple of miles away.

You will notice the name of Ted Ray on the bill. Well, Ted had an engagement up in Liverpool on a Thursday during the run, which meant he had to have the day free. And this meant that for the day Ted was off – a matinee day when there were three performances – a replacement was needed. As the week began, Cissie Williams, the booker, had not yet found a replacement.

It was by a stroke of luck that my agent, Jock Jacobsen, had to take some publicity 'stills' to the Moss Empire's head office in Leicester Square. There he heard Miss Williams wailing to Val Parnell that she couldn't find a name to fill in for Ted Ray.

Jock waited for her to put down the phone and then said, 'Why not let Max Bygraves stand in?' I wasn't of the same stature as Ted Ray, but poor Miss Williams was desperate. 'Where is he?' she asked. Jock told her that I was appearing at Finsbury Park and could possibly make it in a fast taxi. It seemed to be her only hope. Jock hadn't known it was to fill in for *three* performances, but they schemed that with a taxi standing by I could manage the matinee at the Palladium, then rush to Finsbury Park, then a shuttle service to and fro, to and fro . . . But wait a minute. Miss Williams hadn't seen my act. Jock suggested that he take her over to see me doing my stuff at Finsbury Park. It was Monday, so if she didn't like what she saw she could find someone else.

She did like what she saw, so on the Tuesday she brought Val Parnell over to see what *he* thought. He gave the okay.

Every variety performer then dreamed of working the Palladium, the most famous theatre in the world, the zenith, the tops. It was as good as winning an Oscar. I remember the lovely Dorothy Lamour waiting in the wings, ready to go on, on that day when I first stood in for Ted Ray. I was swimming in the wonderful applause as I walked offstage.

She pecked me on the cheek and whispered, 'Young man, you're going places.' I whispered my thanks, then rushed to the waiting taxi. As I sat back, quite unable to take it all in, Jock smiled and said, 'You'll be back.'

I was too – my career changed from 'an act in the sticks' to 'West End artiste', and for the next ten years I was almost resident at that wonderful theatre. I got to know almost every member of the staff by name. Let me tell you about some of it . . .

The poster advertising Dorothy Lamour always brings a glow, especially when I remember her kiss on my cheek.

These posters, sometimes measuring 65 × 20 feet, were pasted up on prime sites all around London and the suburbs. There must have been hundreds of them. And every two weeks bill stickers would paste up new posters publicising the star attractions on the next bill.

The star at the top o' the bill had a fifteen-minute slot. With the overture, that left the support only minutes to do their acts. The sixteen Palladium Tiller Girls were usually on and off in four minutes, Leo de Lyon would follow with four or five minutes and then Ted Ray, an established British comedian, had twelve minutes. There was no time to 'milk' the audience. Heaven help you if you ran over your allotted time – you'd have to deal with an irate stage manager named Jack Matthews who, even as you worked to the audience, was jotting down his daily report that went to the head office of Moss Empire at Leicester Square. These reports were read by Miss Williams, who was responsible for keeping the Moss Empire theatres in Birmingham, Manchester and other big cities supplied with acts and attractions. If you wanted to continue working, it was wise to keep her happy.

I have a friend in Bournemouth, Chris Woodward, who is a professional magician, a very good one too. He is also a walking encyclopedia on the London Palladium. He has made a study of shows and show people who have been involved in that theatre since it was built at the turn of the nineteenth century.

Chris supplied most of the Palladium posters in this book. The early posters were mostly in red, black and white, but around 1952 Day-Glo started being used and that really made people take a second look. The first time I ever saw the wonder of Day-Glo was on a site in Leicester Square. It was something to be seen in daytime, but at night, when car headlights caught the display in their beam, it was stunning, all 18 feet of it.

Michael Bentine and I made a beeline for Leicester Square when we were told about the billboard. After the show we strolled from the Palladium to the Square, then stood on the other side of the road gazing at our names in Day-Glo. A nosy hot-chestnut seller saw us looking at the poster and, taking us for a couple of tourists from overseas, called out, 'That's a bloody good show, that is. That Max is really good.' Still looking at the billboard I asked him, 'Which Max?' He shouted 'Max Miller!', which made Michael Bentine almost choke with laughter. I bought two bags of chestnuts, paid the man half a crown and told him to keep the change. He said, 'Thanks, guv. Enjoy your stay in England.'

There was one of the world's great jugglers on that programme. His name was Rudy Horn and he juggled on a unicycle. His final trick involved balancing six cups and saucers on his head. With the single wheel wobbling – and getting 'oohs and aahs' from the audience – he'd put a suger cube on his foot and, just when the drum roll ended, he'd flick the sugar cube into the air and catch it in the top cup. It was a sensational finish.

There is a saying that if you travel to the top of the Eiffel Tower in Paris, either on the way up or down you invariably meet somebody you know. Two years later, on the way up, who do you think I met in the elevator? You're right – Rudy Horn.

I mentioned earlier that as a youth I gazed in awe at the wonderful Max Miller. Well, now here I was sharing top o' the bill with my idol, and he was talking to me like a father and generously passing on advice. I just listened in admiration. We became good friends.

I must tell you a story that relates to Max Miller. It took

place during the early fifties when I landed a part in the movie *Tom Brown's Schooldays*, as a coachman who conned young Tom Brown about life at Rugby public school. They wanted a bearded rough-speaking Cockney, and yours truly was given the part.

The director, a respected movie-maker named Brian Desmond-Hurst, suggested I grow my own beard rather than spend time in make-up on the days my part was to be filmed.

At the time of shooting I was also appearing at the London Palladium, sharing top billing with 'the one and only' Max Miller. The beard-growing was not a huge success (even now, I can go without shaving for a couple of days with no fear of five o'clock shadow being evident), and with only two weeks to go before filming was to begin, my beard was almost non-existent. I was assured that as long as some bristles were there they could be darkened. So I persevered and hoped the make-up department could do the rest.

After the show at the Palladium one evening, Max Miller invited me into his dressing room for a drink. You must remember that my admiration for this man then was the same as my three grandsons' adulation for Tiger Woods today. Max Miller seemed to know more about the art and the secrets of show business than any other person I had met. At that time he was a *BIG* star, so if he had a theory or thought about the complex skills of a solo performer, you listened.

As we chatted, Max leaned closer and enquired, 'Have you shaved today?' I told him I hadn't shaved for almost a week, because of my upcoming film appearance in *Tom Brown's Schooldays*. Max gave me a little advice that has stayed with me. He leaned forward and recommended that I get clean shaven as soon as possible, adding, 'No man ever got laughs, or won an audience over, with hair on his face – ever!'

How true this is. Over the years I have seen colleagues try

the bearded approach and then, after a few appearances, go back to the open face, clean shaven. These include John Cleese, Peter Ustinov, Jimmy Tarbuck, Bill Maynard, Michael Bentine, Peter Sellers and quite a few more.

When I eventually filmed my part in the Tom Brown epic, the director allowed me to settle for sideburns, not the full beard. Several years later, in the same theatre, the Palladium, I introduced the Beatles in a Royal Variety Show. Just before they went on stage John Lennon said to me, 'Like my sideburns? I copied them from you in *Tom Brown's Schooldays.*' I didn't like to tell him my side whiskers had been glued on with spirit gum – he'd have thought it was a bare-faced lie.

Reading the list on this bill of support for Donald Peers (see colour plate), I can see it was packed with entertainers of the highest quality. Juggler José Moreno, a Spaniard, did things with a ball that would have made David Beckham envious. He was the best. His attractive wife was his assistant and kept him supplied with balls and clubs. She always got lots of wolf whistles from the audience. With the biggest smile, she would wink back at them.

Another great scene-stealing act on the bill was the Nicholas Brothers, two fast rhythmic dancers from Harlem. Before this appearance they had only been seen in movies in the UK. They looked like teenagers but had been around for ever.

They were followed in the first half by Ethel Smith, a swing organist who had become famous for the dexterity of her fingers at the organ keyboard. Val Parnell figured that fifteen minutes of organ playing might bore the audience, so he called for a choreographer to 'tart it up' by bringing on the Tiller Girls for a dance routine to Miss Smith's 'Tico Tico'. The girls were turned out like Carmen Miranda, and their efforts earned Ethel Smith twice the amount of applause.

I did well in my spot, second after the interval, after which came the star attraction, Donald Peers. He had an accompanist named Ernest Ponticelli, whom I was pals with. Ernest later went on to work in Tin Pan Alley at a music publishing firm, plugging music. He had a bad time with his eyesight and died comparatively young.

Donald had a rather painful end. He'd gone to Australia to perform, in a theatre where they'd set up a makeshift stage by pushing two large rostrums together. Unfortunately there was a discrepancy in their height. Donald told me that his heel had slipped as he walked on stage, only an inch or so, but it had injured his back. The discs had been stripped, which caused him unbelievable pain. He'd had to fly back (in those days more than thirty hours), and when I saw him in a Manchester hospital he could hardly move. He died shortly after.

In these days of suing, he would probably have been compensated for a large amount, but he died in poor circumstances and with very little fanfare.

The following April I was booked for the Judy Garland season at the Palladium. By then *Educating Archie* on the BBC had become their most popular programme. We were winning awards and all of us were becoming star names. My billing at the Palladium and at other theatres was becoming larger and more prominent.

At the time I was performing a different song every week on the *Educating Archie* broadcasts. I was also touring variety theatres the length and breadth of Britain. I wasn't experienced enough then to explain to the bandleader at these dates how I wanted my accompaniment played. I hadn't yet learned the word 'segue', which was what I wanted for going into a chorus without stopping and sometimes changing the key on the way. I didn't know how to tell the band to attack an ending by saying 'forte' or 'crescendo', and words like 'pianissimo' were Greek to me (I later found out they are Latin). Then I met Bob Dixon who became my musical director, and my worries were over. I certainly learned a lot from him.

Musicians come in all shapes and sizes: long hair, longer hair, dyed hair; smokers, drinkers, drug addicts; studious, slobs, refined slobs – you name it. Bob was a gentleman. He wasn't a good teacher. In fact he was rather mean with musical advice. But he had the touch of a genius once his hands caressed the piano keyboard. Like me he had served in the RAF and played with the station band. 'Did you have to carry the piano whilst on the march?' I once kidded him. He looked at me and then as if explaining to a child, he said, 'I played the f. . ...g cymbals!'

In his Lancashire dialect, which he never lost in the 36 years we worked together, there was never a bad word between us. When I once told this to bandleader Billy Cotton, Bob interrupted to say, 'Why should there be? I have the world's highest-paid chauffeur [*me!*]; I get picked up and dropped off. I'm paid each week, work or not, and all I have to do is do what I do best – play the piano.'

When asked by one of the music papers to write a piece on our association, I wrote the following:

Bob Dixon was my accompanist for more than 36 years and I still can't get used to the idea that he is not behind me on stage appearances, tinkling away at the piano. We had a silent code going on between us: if an audience was not on our wavelength, I would switch channels – that is, go to a totally different routine to the one rehearsed. He would know I had changed gear and would be ready to play, even if it were a piece that we hadn't performed for ten years or more. He had a photographic memory and could rattle off things like credits on an old movie – sometimes he'd even remember who did the make-up.

He could do *The Times* crossword in half an hour and was an authority on sport. And he could drink – never before a show, but as soon as the curtain came down he would make the nearest bar faster than Sebastian Coe.

He came from Ulverston in Lancashire. Although we travelled the length and breadth of Britain, with twenty-odd trips around the world, he never lost his northern accent. In fact, it got more pronounced over the years.

A short, balding figure, which earned him the nick-name Mr Sheen, he was the most loyal and conscientious worker I have ever known. One thing he was not was technically minded.

We were in Perth, Australia. I walked into his dressing room just before a show one evening and saw him getting ready to shave. His face was lathered and he was trying to fit a three-holed safety razor he'd used back in his RAF days many moons before.

I told him he was wasting his time with that sort of razor, that there was a new plastic one on the market called BIC, which was disposable. 'I'll get you some next time I go to the chemist's,' I said. A few days later, I purchased a packet of half a dozen and gave them to him.

That same night, he walked into my dressing room and said: 'Them bloody razors wouldn't cut butter hot!' He still had the lather on his face, the razor in his hand. I looked at it and said, 'You have to take the orange plastic cover off before it works.'

He had been trying to use it with the safety cover on. After he had removed that and tried, he was more impressed. 'Where's the blade?' he asked, then ran his finger along the sharp edge to see. He cut his finger.

It was only a small cut, but as he said at the time, 'I'm an easy bleeder.' Later, a couple of stagehands were shifting the piano Bob had played and saw that the keyboard was covered in blood. One of them said, 'Who's been playing this – Dracula?' We got one of the St John's ladies from the front of the theatre to try to stem the flow of blood, but to no avail. We were 'on' in a few minutes.

My act usually lasts for more than an hour. When the curtain eventually came down, I walked over to the piano and saw that there was blood all over the keyboard. We had to get Bob to hospital straightaway. Meanwhile the blood wouldn't stop flowing. It was one of the dancing girls who came up with an idea to stop the bleeding. She improvised a large, white finger stool.

In the car going to the hospital Bob asked where the finger stool had come from. It was hard to tell him that it was fashioned from what ladies use when that time of the month comes round.

We waited at the outpatients for a good hour or more. Eventually a doctor appeared, a know-all who had obviously been imbibing and was annoyed at being called for duty past midnight. He said to Bob, 'And what the hell's up with you?'

Bob bristled, held up his finger and, in broad Lancashire, said, 'I'm 'aving a fooking bad period!'

*

The fifties, especially the early part, were the time when Great Britain was getting back on its feet. Rationing was almost finished, there was work for all, the pubs were doing capacity business, and the tills in the box offices of music halls and theatres were ringing merrily.

There was a surge of talent – people who had been in the services and had decided to try to break into show business – not only in the big cities but at concert parties in seaside towns and in long-running pantomimes. I was among this new wave.

There were those who took the easy route, by following the style of the older performers who were still topping bills up and down the country. But what most of us were striving for was to be different, to express our own personality.

I discovered a style that drew attention. It was hard to get the audience to accept at first, but I stuck with it. As I became more confident, agents and bookers turned up at theatres to see what I was all about. What I had figured out was that most of us new to the game, who were allotted just nine or ten minutes for our act, would rush onto the stage as if we were eager to get it over with. I used a different approach: I sauntered on stage, pulling a bentwood chair behind me. When I reached centre stage I reversed the chair to face the audience and, after I had made myself comfortable, I spoke my first line to the audience. It was cheeky but it worked a treat.

I'd say to them, 'Well – you're all sitting.' Then, instead of rushing the dialogue, I'd take my time. After about three minutes I'd tell the audience I was going to tell a joke, and would they please laugh, otherwise the management would find other work for me. I'd then tell a joke that purposely 'died'. A stagehand would walk across the stage, hand me a broom and walk off, after which I'd start sweeping, muttering to myself lines like, 'They told me if I played this theatre I'd *clean up!*'', which got a nervous laugh. Then I'd look off stage and say to the stagehand (unseen), 'Listen to that – that deserves more than a broom, doesn't it?' A bucket and mop would be thrown on from the opposite side of stage.

I'd pick up the pail and mop, telling the audience, 'Before I kick the bucket . . . I would like to do my impression of Charles Boyer.' Using the mop as if it were a girl, as Boyer I'd whisper, 'Hedy, Hedy.' I'd make the mop tremble, adding 'Hedy, steady!'

On paper this sounds trite, but let me tell you, it was that sort of material that was going to put me on the road to success, not only in the UK but around the world. It was something different, something the others weren't doing. I used it for quite a few years at the beginning of my vaudeville days. Don't forget that at the time I was a happy young fellow who could carry a tune. All I had to do was come up with ideas that registered.

Then I met Eric Sykes. It was at the Camberwell Palace. Frankie Howerd had just completed another winner for the BBC and the Beeb was honouring him by supplying drink and sandwiches for the cast and technicians. Eric was being violently ill in the ladies' toilet backstage.

I didn't know it at the time but Eric felt rather hard done by. Back in those days script writers rarely got much credit for their work. The illusion the BBC kept up was that Frankie Howerd was more or less making it all up as he went along. But I knew he had a good writer, and I asked Frank to give me his name. It turned out to be Eric Sykes.

The reason Sykes was in the ladies loo, bringing his lunch up, was because the measly £5 the Beeb was paying him for these wonderful routines just wasn't enough. On this particular night he had decided to make up for it by helping himself to some of the drink. Unfortunately he wasn't able to hold his liquor. When I found him he was bent double over the bowl. I asked if he was all right and helped him to make his way to the gents. There I told Eric I had come to see him on the recommendation of Mr Howerd. He confessed he felt too ill to talk, but gave me his phone number and the address of his digs, which at the time was in Earls Court Road.

My wife, who was disgusted with this moron who had left the ladies' loo in an appalling state, begged me not to get mixed up with him. But I kept his phone number.

When I turned up at his one room in Earls Court he invited me in and asked if I would like a cup of tea. I said I would. He asked me to hang on as he was boiling an egg in the only saucepan he had, and would I mind if he used the same water to make the tea. I told him it was okay. It was the start of a friendship that has lasted more than fifty years.

It wasn't long before the BBC realised what original and humorous scripts Sykes was turning out, and rewarded him by making him co-writer of a new series to be titled *Educating Archie*.

By then I was making movies at Bushey with a comedian named Hal Monty. The producer Arthur Dent was a lovely gentleman, who I think hailed from South Africa. Sometimes I would mimic Mr Dent for Eric. This amused Eric so much that when he was given the job on *Educating Archie* he

STARS IN MY EYES ☆

suggested I play the part of Archie's tutor. I kept Mr Dent's delivery in mind.

At the end of the first series, I had become the king of the catchphrase in Britain. I think I had more going for me than the wonderful Tommy Handley – phrases like 'A good idea, son!', 'I've arrived, and to prove it I'm 'ere!' and 'Big 'ead Dollar lolly!' were some of the ones that established me as an entertainer.

When I look back at that radio programme, I can recall the small room where the cast would sit. It is hard to believe that in that room where we rehearsed the dialogue written by Eric were people who were later to be so famous – stars like Tony Hancock, Julie Andrews, Beryl Reid, Eric Sykes and Hattie Jacques as well as Peter Brough. We were all doing well, talking to a block of wood! Even now it's hard to convince some of the youngsters that the star of the show on radio was a ventriloquist's dummy called Archie Andrews.

Incidentally, my wife Blossom adores Eric now.

The next bill I worked on was with the one and only Judy Garland. It was a packed house, with the audience ready to be entertained and to love her, when something happened to ruin her well-rehearsed entrance.

With the microphone in her hand and the lead trailing behind her, Judy came on smiling, saying 'Thank you'. Then she stepped backwards over the microphone lead and crashed down, as she later said, 'full on my fan'. It was a most unladylike entrance. She ran for the wings, screaming, 'Oh my God, oh my God, I slipped . . .' Jack Matthews put his arm around her and gently said, 'It's all right, they love you. Listen to them. They don't care about your trip.' Meanwhile, the band was still going round and round with the intro to 'The Trolley Song'.

Judy walked back on stage, kicked off her high-heeled shoes and murmured, 'I certainly fell for you!' – probably one of the best ad libs I have ever heard in a situation like

53

this. The crowd roared its approval, and Judy was home. She was a fantastic hit and would continue to be for the many times she came to our shores.

Above *The Peep Show* with Anthony in the sixties.

Above right Fishing in Sydney with grandson Michael… you can tell he didn't like fishing with worms.

Right Maxine, my daughter, is in the middle. I am the one in the cap.

Above Joan
Regan and Alma
Cogan singing
Joan's baby
to sleep.

Right A publicity
still with my
family – '*Olé*',
which means
'with milk!'.

HOMEWARD BOUND—FROM MAJORCA

Left Our 40th wedding anniversary – Blossom still not showing the strain.

Below Blossom still as happy.

Below My first Oscar – he is now an undergraduate at Oxford.

Below right With my mother in Glasgow – as you can see, the birds were happy enough…

Above Eamonn says, 'My life – this is yours.'

Right An award from Reader's Digest for 'Singalonga Max' albums.

'I wanna tell you a story.'

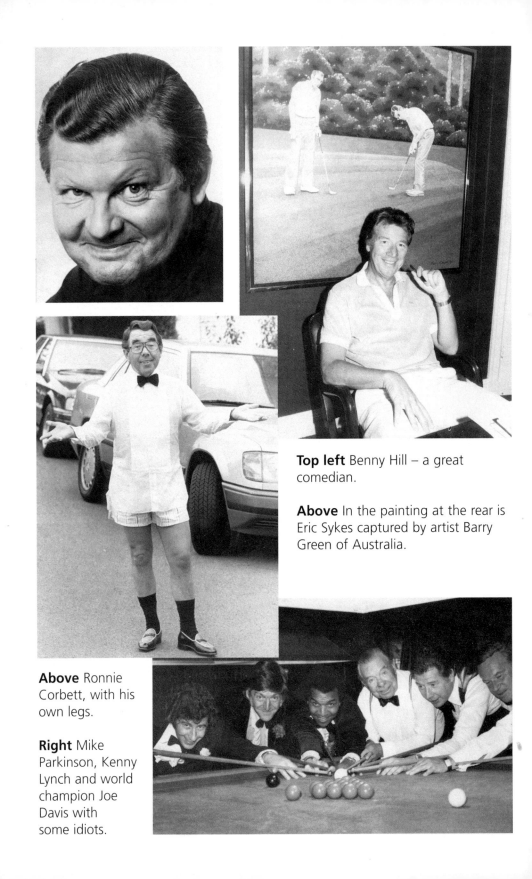

Top left Benny Hill – a great comedian.

Above In the painting at the rear is Eric Sykes captured by artist Barry Green of Australia.

Above Ronnie Corbett, with his own legs.

Right Mike Parkinson, Kenny Lynch and world champion Joe Davis with some idiots.

With two beauties: my Rolls
and model Beverley.

Above Among the line-up were Dickie Henderson, Jim Davidson, Mike Yarwood and Bruce Forsyth – oh, and er… His Highness.

Below It was debatable who had the bigger bouffant, Shirley Bassey or Lord Delfont.

AGENTS

In our business agents are sometimes referred to as 'ten-percenters'. Should you become a sought-after attraction, the agent need only pick up the phone and arrive at a price for the next engagement. Once this is passed on to the client, the agent starts collecting his percentage, and usually ropes in a fee from the booker too.

If an artiste happens to get into a long-running show he pays the agent ten per cent for the entire engagement. There are some shows running in London's West End that started in the eighties. So you can see how lucrative a long run can be to an agent.

Stories about agents abound. There's one about two agents sitting in a theatre watching the performers on stage. One agent turns to the other and says, 'Look at those so and so's – taking ninety per cent of our money.'

Another story is about a well-known agent who is angling to get a lot more performers on his books. At a theatre in London he sees an amazing acrobatic act that 'brings the house down'. The act is so good the agent goes backstage to talk business with the performer. He says, 'You were superb – the greatest act I have seen in all my years. How much are you getting?' The acrobat tells him, and the agent says, 'What! Is that all you're getting? I could get you four times that amount. Who is your agent?' The acrobat replies, 'You are.'

I had the same agent for 36 years. His name was Jock Jacobsen. When we first agreed for him to represent me he had one room in a block at the back of Trafalgar Square, and travelled to the office on the underground. When he left this earth 36 years later he drove a Rolls Royce.

Over that time, his agency grew and his 'stable' of performers became more select. He was respected throughout the business, thoughtful, kind, full of know how and always a pleasure to be with. Jock was a *good* agent, not a ten-percenter.

STARS AND STRIPES IN MY EYES

Jock Jacobsen was to be instrumental in the next period of my life. I was finding that being a regular performer can be very restrictive, especially if you are continually playing London's West End. This is because you start to have a following that is always wanting new ideas, new gags, new songs. You think you are doing the best you'll ever do and that you don't need a new act – if you had a better one you'd be doing it! You start to get the feeling that what you need to be a 'stayer' is a new audience.

I was in this sort of situation when a phone call came from Los Angeles. It was Judy Garland. She told me she was opening at the Palace on Times Square in New York, and she wanted me as support. Would I come?

Would I come! Wow!! She wanted me to do the same act I had performed when I was on the bill with her at the Palladium. I couldn't think of another patter act like myself ever before working on Broadway, and the thought of performing to a brand new audience made me tingle – not with fear, but with good old excitement.

Jock sorted out the monetary side with Sid Luft, who was Judy's manager, getting me four times the salary I was earning at the Palladium. A few weeks later I was aboard a BOAC Comet on my way to New York. In those days it took fourteen hours, with stops for refuelling at Goose Bay. I slept almost all the way, Jock sitting beside me wide awake. He often told the story of our first Atlantic flight, adding that I was fearless. He, on the other hand, compared himself to Colonel Lindbergh, the first solo flyer to cross the Atlantic, who was awake for the entire flight. Of course, Jock had counted every cloud throughout the flight while grasping the arm rests with white knuckles. On landing, I remarked that it had been a great smooth flight. Jock replied, 'How would you know?'

No wonder Sinatra was always plugging 'New York, New York is a wonderful town . . .' It was everything I had expected from the black and white movies I had seen in the past – but *this* was in full colour.

One of the first things I did was to go to the top of the Empire State Building, at that time the highest building in the world. You've got to believe that as a boy from London's East End dockland, looking out at that skyline and suburbs was just about the greatest thrill I had known in my 28 years. A few days later we opened at the Palace – on my birthday, 16 October 1950. Happy birthday, Max? Yes, indeed.

Judy was a smash hit – the press had nothing but praise for this Hollywood star who was 'even better in the flesh'. She was deservedly the biggest thing to hit Broadway for many a year. Her success rubbed off onto the other acts, and we were all a smash.

The people who called backstage were mostly well-known personalities, and the stars in my eyes were making me twinkle. Clark Gable, Bob Hope, Danny Kaye, Jack Benny, James Mason, Frank Sinatra, June Allyson and Dick

Powell, and many more, all being lavish with praise when I was introduced to them. Twinkle, twinkle!

There's a story I love to tell about Judy at the Palace. It has to do with Walter Winchell, who was probably the most powerful columnist in America during the early fifties. (If you ever watched the television series *The Untouchables*, you will remember the staccato-voiced narration; this was delivered by Walter Winchell.) He wrote a complimentary line about me in his column while I was appearing at the Palace with Judy, and because of that one line the phone in my hotel room hardly stopped ringing. Top agents MCA wanted me on their books, as did the William Morris Agency. I was wooed by almost the entire show business scene, yet all he said as far as I can remember was: 'Max Bygraves – funny man from England puts paid to the rumour that Englishmen have no sense of humour. Don't miss him . . .'

Winchell started life in vaudeville and had been a hoofer. How he gave it up to become the most important show-biz newspaper man in the US I don't know, but he was and remained so for his lifetime. Most people in American show business would have shot their grandmothers for an inch or two in his column, and Judy Garland was no exception.

We performed two shows daily at the Palace – a matinee at 2.30 plus an evening performance at 8. Most of the theatrical and press people came to the afternoon show. Every performance was a sell-out and tickets were as difficult to get as for the men's finals at Wimbledon.

The show had been running for several weeks when one Wednesday matinee the buzz went round backstage: 'Winchell's in!' Even the stagehands moved twice as fast.

Wearing the fedora he was famed for, he made his entrance to the Stalls, removing the hat only when the lights went down for the overture. By now the entire audience was aware that the great one was in their midst.

With two or more songs still to go, Judy decided to

introduce Winchell to the crowd. They cheered, and when those in the Upper Circle loudly complained they could not see him, he cheerfully left his seat and walked towards the orchestra pit so those above could have a better view. Judy enticed him onto the stage to thunderous applause. He was beaming and loving every moment as the spotlight picked him out.

Judy told him how thrilled she was to have him on stage, and they threw compliments at each other. Then Winchell surprised Judy by telling her that he had worked on this very stage before, as a dancer. She was genuinely surprised and asked what sort of dancing he did. Winchell asked the musical director for a stop chorus of 'Bye Bye Blues', a standard for most dancers, and the roof almost fell in as New York's favourite reporter went into a 'buck and wing'. I stood on the side of the stage watching all this, and couldn't believe the standing ovation they gave him for these few simple steps. They cheered him all the way back to his seat. Anything Judy attempted after was an anticlimax – it was a case of 'follow that!'

Two days go by and Winchell turns up again, but this time with a couple of friends. Slowly the Judy Garland Show is becoming the Walter Winchell Show, and Judy isn't too pleased at the way things are going. Something has to be done.

Sid Luft, Judy's manager who later became her husband, hit on the idea of telling Winchell that the Musicians' Union were not allowed to play for any performer who was not a card-carrying Union man. He showed Winchell a letter on MU notepaper that testified to this.

The write-ups on Judy stopped from that moment. Judy was sad but relieved.

Years later, when Winchell had passed away, I met Sid Luft in Bond Street. As we strolled towards Piccadilly, we talked about the Winchell episode. 'It was a good thing the Musicians' Union sent that letter, wasn't it Sid?' He replied,

'It was a good thing my brother-in-law was not only the musical director but the Union representative and had some headed notepaper that we could use, otherwise Winchell would have been on till the day he died!'

In New York, like any other city, the shopkeepers and café owners near the theatre were thrilled at the business we were generating. One place, a café called Gus and Andy's, recognised me from the posters and thereafter would never take payment for my coffee and salt beef sandwich, always greeting me with 'Shalom'.

A shoe-shine man I was on nodding terms with would sit outside the Palace doing a brisk trade. One day he pointed to my suede shoes, which I had purchased at Macy's, saying, 'Suede shoes should not be worn in the city.' He made this remark each time I passed his pitch. 'Why shouldn't suede shoes be worn in the city?' I asked him. 'Because it's no good for my f. . ...g business,' he retorted.

One matinee, Elizabeth Taylor, Montgomery Clift and Frank Sinatra were sitting in the front stalls. The two men had just appeared together in a blockbuster movie *From Here to Eternity*, and they were really enjoying the show. I closed the first half, then remarked to the stage manager how thrilling it was to see such big stars sitting together in the audience. 'It proves something,' he said. When I asked him what, he said, 'It proves they're all outta work.'

The place to eat was the famous Lindy's, and after the show that's where most of the show-biz crowd hung out – mostly comedians working at nightclubs near Times Square. I made many friends there but one in particular was Danny Kaye. I knew him fairly well in London, but in his home town he was God.

During the run in New York, sworn to secrecy, we were all told to be at the home of Richard Rodgers (of Rodgers and Hammerstein fame) one Sunday evening at 7.30 p.m. sharp. The entire cast was invited, plus some musicians and male dancers, some thirty in all. We were told it was a surprise party for Judy, because Richard Rodgers wanted to say a 'thank you' to her.

When our 'lookout' said the taxi with Sid Luft and Judy had arrived, all lights were switched off and we were told to hide and keep quiet. We heard the key Sid had been given turn in the lock and then Judy exclaimed, 'Sid, where the hell is the light switch?' There was an almighty crash as Judy bumped into a glass cabinet, followed by the sort of language usually spoken by drunken sailors but on this night delivered expletively by Judy G.

The lights went on to 'Surprise, surprise!' A red-faced Judy collapsed with laughter, adding 'Oh sh..t!' We all stayed until after midnight – it was some party.

When the New York run finished, *The Judy Garland Show* went to Hollywood, and me with it. Although I was feeling on top of the world, performing live in the heart of the movie world, I found 'tinsel town' to be an apt description for Hollywood – for me it glittered.

It was Sid Luft, then married to Judy, who suggested I should get myself a press agent. Sid convinced me to use a fellow he knew well. For two hundred dollars a week he would get snippets of gossip about me in the *Hollywood Reporter*, the *Los Angeles Times*, *Variety* and various other publications.

Like a muggins I took on this press agent, only to read things I had never said or done – things like: 'Max Bygraves, British performer with *The Judy Garland Show*, turned down an offer when the salesman told him "they stand by every bed they sell".'

People familiar with Americanisms told me it was a very funny joke, but I didn't think it was all that clever. There were others that I didn't understand. I was supposed to have uttered, 'Wanna try a Mulligan?' Apparently a 'Mulligan' in golf talk meant 'another go'. I decided to drop this press agent and save myself the money.

I don't know what it's like now in Hollywood, but back

in the fifties it wasn't unusual to find yourself rubbing shoulders with some of the biggest names around. Once at the Hollywood Roosevelt Hotel I found myself in the elevator with Richard Widmark. And at The Brown Derby, a restaurant I ate in regularly, on my way to my table one evening I passed George Burns with his wife Gracie Allen, Jack Benny and his wife Mary, Alfred Hitchcock, Janis Paige and Humphrey Bogart. Another star encounter came when I made a call to my American agents MCA, who had offices on Santa Monica Boulevard.

My car, a rented Chevrolet, was parked in the clients' car park. When I returned, I found a small black and chrome MG blocking me in. The two-seater MG was at such an angle it would have been impossible for me to back out without damaging it. As I stood there scratching my head, trying to figure out what to do, a voice behind me said, 'Looks like I've fenced you in.' It was Clark Gable. He was exactly as if the silver screen had come to life – same smile, moustache, check jacket, canary yellow turtleneck pullover and staccato voice. 'What are we gonna do?' he asked. I told him that if he got into the MG and reversed very carefully we could solve the problem without any paint being scraped.

He listened to me, then asked, 'Are you English?' I told him I was, and he gave me his keys, saying, 'Here, you get it out. It's an English car.'

I got into the driving seat, started the engine and very, very slowly backed the MG out safely. He said, 'Nice work. What're you doing in Hollywood?' I told him I was appearing in *The Judy Garland Show* in Los Angeles. He seemed very interested, and then I remembered that Judy had done a memorable bit in a musical movie where she sang 'You Made Me Love You' to a photograph of Clark Gable. 'Hey! Give my love to Judy, will yer?' he said as he drove off. 'And if you're near the lot over at MGM, come and say hello.' Oh, how I wish my boyhood chum in Rotherhithe had been near at hand. Willie Perkins would never have been able to top that encounter with Clark Gable like he once did with Errol Flynn opening a taxi door.

James Mason became a good friend, and often invited Blossom and me and our three children to his house on Rodeo Drive. There I would be dazzled by his other guests. It was at Mason's house that an unforgettable episode took place. I often relate this story – it sounds like name-dropping but is perfectly true and still makes me shudder. I was by the pool talking to James Mason and Frank Sinatra. Ava Gardner, who was there with Frank, was in the main house – there had been 'words' and Miss Gardner was sitting in the lounge, sobbing her heart out. Frank was telling us that she would get over it, when I noticed Mason's eyes grow wide. Fully clothed he jumped into the pool and waded quickly over to a tiny figure struggling with an inflatable ring, the kind that children use in pools. When the youngster came to the surface I could see it was my five-year-old son, Anthony.

His legs were caught up in the ring, and it was only James Mason's quickness that had rescued him from drowning. What can one say in a situation like that? When Anthony had got his breath back I told him to go over to James and say, 'Thank you for saving my life.' This really amused both Mason and Sinatra. Mason's lovely wife, Pamela, told Anthony not to do it again because the clothes dryer had fused and there was nowhere to dry her husband's clothes.

Ava Gardner appeared and gave Frank a big wet kiss. Everybody clapped them and we all went home.

Another stalwart of show business whom I got to know intimately around that time was Jack Benny. Jack would take me to Hillcrest Golf Club, an exclusive course near Beverly Hills. There is a large table overlooking the eighteenth green that is reserved for the show-biz fraternity. Almost any day you could find stars like Danny Thomas, George Burns, Groucho Marx, Bob Hope and more, topping each others' jokes. It was here I was to meet and become friends with a pal of Jack's, George Burns.

When I asked George to fly from LA to London to be a guest on my TV programme *LingalongaMax*, I expected him to beg off, because of age – but not a bit of it. With his manager, Irving Fein, he made the trip with ease. When I met him at Heathrow, he looked fit enough to take on Muhammad Ali, and he was nearly eighty then! George just went on and on, reaching just past his hundredth birthday. I was saddened to see him go.

When Jack Benny and George Burns were together, it was like having a front seat at a great vaudeville show. One evening, a group of us were having dinner at Chasen's in Beverly Hills, a restaurant frequented by many of the big Hollywood stars. George tapped my knee under the table to signal to me he was about to play a joke on Jack. He lit a fresh cigar, then said, 'Jack, we have been coming to this restaurant for twenty years. Many people come in just to stare at us, and at other times we have brought large parties with us. Yet not once has the owner ever said, "Have this dinner on me – I'll pay the bill".' Jack agreed that Dave Chasen had never picked up the tab.

George continued: 'Tonight when he brings the bill, whoever he gives it to, let the other one of us say, "I'll pay that." If Dave then gives it to the other one of us, the first person should say, "If he pays that bill I will never use this restaurant again." The other person should say, "And if *he* pays it, *I* will never come here again!" Dave will be so embarrassed he will have to tear the goddam bill up.'

After coffee, Dave Chasen came to the table and placed the bill in front of George Burns. Jack immediately said, 'If you let him pay that bill, I will never come into this restaurant again.' Chasen picked up the check and laid it in front of Jack, whereupon George just went on puffing his cigar, looking at the ceiling. Jack fell about laughing as he realised that he had been set up by Burns – George had phoned earlier and arranged it. They had dozens more of these elaborate jokes, and they were the greatest of pals.

Jack was to have starred in *The Sunshine Boys*, but he died before it was ready for shooting. So Irving Fein secured the part for George and it started a new movie career for him.

One of George's lines that stays with me is when he was talking about the death of Eddie Cantor. Somebody asked if he left much, and George replied, 'Everything.'

Many years later, I was to meet one of the diners whom I had seen often in Chasen's restaurant, the director Alfred Hitchcock. It seems he had seen me in a movie.

Hitchcock was very well respected in the movie world, and almost any actor was happy to be directed by him. You can imagine that when he showed an interest in my work I was overwhelmed. He had seen a movie I made in the fifties, called *Cry from the Streets*, and had liked what he'd seen, so he sent for me to come to his office at 139 Piccadilly. He wanted to see me alone, with no manager or agent, just the two of us for a talk (and he loved to talk).

I arrived a few minutes before our appointment, which was for 2.30 p.m. Right on the stroke of the half hour, a secretary took me into the room where the great man was seated at a very large desk. There was an empty seat facing him, where he told me to sit. 'Good afternoon, Mr Bygraves. How nice of you to come.' His enunciation was like a send-up of himself. I wanted to answer in the same voice, 'The pleasure is all mine', but instead I thanked him in what I hoped was my natural-sounding delivery for the pleasure of his company.

He didn't take his eyes off me, and asked me about the movies I had made. Did I enjoy them? How long did they take to produce? Did they do well at the box office? I told him the answers, while thinking that I was talking to the man who had directed some of the 'greats', from Ray Milland and Cary Grant to James Stewart, Sean Connery and so many more.

I wasn't nervous in his company, just 'keyed up'. I

decided to ask him about *his* work, thinking that even if nothing came from the interview, even if I didn't get the part, at least I could boast about questions I had asked *him*.

It was not hard. I asked how he had filmed the aerial shot of Cary Grant being chased by the aeroplane in *North by Northwest*, and also how he got the collection of black crows to attack Tippi Hendren in *The Birds*.

He enjoyed answering the latter question: 'There were two ladies, now retired, who had worked many years for the Walt Disney Company. They had also worked on *Wizard of Oz* as artists making film effects. I traced them and asked them to come out of retirement to help me with some work on *The Birds*. On plain paper, with no background, I got them to paint the crows in close-up and in flight. I photographed these on to backgrounds I was using with live flocks of birds. It was that easy.'

He folded his arms across his ample stomach, as if to say 'It was nothing really'. We chatted some more, and then he told me I had got the part in a picture to be called *Frenzy*. I left the office in Piccadilly walking on air. It was five o'clock, which meant we had chatted for two and a half hours. Before I left he gave me an inkling as to how he worked. He said, 'I have this large spool of film, and use every frame of film – very little goes on the cutting room floor. I rarely do retakes – that is a stupid way to make films.' I nodded understandingly. What Mr Hitchcock was saying to me was, when you turn up for work, know your lines, be professional and don't waste time. He didn't put it that way, but that was his meaning.

There is a sad ending to this story. A few weeks after the meeting, I had to go to Manchester where I was booked to appear in cabaret at a venue known as the Golden Garter. It was during my two weeks there that Alfred Hitchcock wanted to film night shots in Covent Garden. There was no way I could get the date altered. All my shows were sold out and it would have been impossible to return the booking money. So I lost the part. Alfred Hitchcock sent word that he would keep me in mind for something else, but he didn't make another movie – *Frenzy* was his last. He died peacefully in Hollywood.

BY ROYAL COMMAND

If asked who has been the biggest, most memorable and joyous star I have had the good fortune to meet during my long career, it would always be the same answer: our queen, Her Majesty Queen Elizabeth II.

Never have I ever toyed with the idea of returning my OBE medal to grab an inch or two of space in some tabloid. I am as proud as any other Britisher who has had the honour bestowed. I felt this pride the first time I performed before King George VI in 1950 and later, in 1952, for Her Majesty, and I have tingled every time since. To be there 'doing my stuff' in front of that wonderful presence is a thrill. She's a shining star that puts any other star into the forty-watt category.

Almost anybody who has met this lovely lady remembers every word spoken. No matter how brief, they will repeat and repeat the words she spoke. My wife Blossom was impressed by the concern expressed by HM when first spoken to at Windsor Castle. I was there as one of the entertainers performing in the ballroom for the Royal Family and staff. There were just two seats in front of the stage, which were occupied by HM and Princess Margaret; the rest were sitting on the ballroom floor.

It was at the time when a very young Prince Charles was at Gordonstoun school and had been found drinking cherry brandy. The newspapers were having a field day reporting on the schoolboy 'drunk'. This harmless sip of cherry brandy was great fodder for comics, including me, a way to get easy laughs. 'Prince Charles is working on a new comedy act with W C Fields [a well-known imbiber], to be known as Handy and Brandy.' An awful joke, I know, but under the circumstances a real crowd-pleaser, as was: 'At Gordonstoun they've done away with the eleven plus. They now do the breathalyser test.'

Later, when HM and my wife Bloss were having a 'natter', the question of young Charles came up – both being mothers with sons almost the same age. HM wished the press 'would leave him alone and stop hounding the poor chap'.

*

I have wonderful memories of Royal Command Performances, and many stories, usually stories that rarely reached the ears of the public. Over the years, of course, these stories get embellished with re-telling. There is one 'story' that supposedly concerned my friend Tommy Cooper. It was the 1953 RCP, the first attended by our new young queen, and a star-studded event that included big names of the day – apart from myself waiting in the wings there were Eamonn Andrews, Eve Boswell, Jimmy Edwards, the Hastings Girls Choir, Dick James, Anne Shelton, the cast from *Guys and Dolls* plus a dozen supporting acts . . . and Tommy Cooper.

After the performance, the story goes, Tommy was talking to Her Majesty in the line-up:

TC: 'Excuse me, ma'm, do you like football?'

HM: 'No, not very much.'

TC: 'You like it a little bit, don't you ma'm?'

HM: 'No, I don't like football at all.'

TC: 'But you'd go to see a top class game, wouldn't you?'

HM (shaking her head): 'No.'

TC: 'Well, ma'am, can I have your tickets for the Cup Final?'

Now, told right it is a very funny story – but it was never uttered by Tommy Cooper. It goes back to Bud Flanagan of Flanagan and Allen many years before, when he was talking to the Queen Mum. I must admit it goes over better done in Tommy's delivery, but the credit does belong to Bud Flanagan.

*

Command Performance night can be nerve-racking to most performers, whether big or small names. The big names in their own shows know that when a customer buys a ticket they do so because they want to see that performer. At a Royal Command show, where some tickets cost an arm and a leg, an artiste is never sure whether the audience knows or likes them, so everybody from the top to the bottom walks onstage with apprehension. Let me tell you a story about Bud Flanagan and Norman Wisdom . . .

It was Norman's very first Royal Command Performance, and he was nervous. I was a little cocky because I had already appeared in a couple of RCPs. On these shows dressing-room space is at a premium so acts have to share. This particular show I had to share with Norman, plus a comedian named Arthur Haynes and The Crazy Gang.

Bud Flanagan noticed the nail-biting Norman, and took him aside. 'What are you worried about?' Bud asked. 'I've never done one of these before. What if they don't like me?' Norman replied. Bud put his arm around Norman's shoulder and said, 'Look son, you are here because you are the best. If there was anyone better than you, you wouldn't be here, they would!'

I watched as the words sank in. Then Bud, who like me had done his part in the first half, invited me for a drink at the pub across the road. In the meantime Norman went on and stormed the audience, backed by the Billy Cotton Band. The audience cheered his efforts, and the Queen found him 'hilarious'.

After the interval, I wandered back from my drink with Bud Flanagan. I walked into the dressing room, to find a flushed and happy Norman Wisdom and a worried Arthur Haynes, who had yet to appear in his spot. There was Norman Wisdom with his arm around nervous Arthur Haynes, saying, 'Look pal, you are here because you are the best. If there was anyone better than you, you wouldn't be here, they would.' I didn't make my presence known and quietly slipped away.

That RCP was my first meeting with the much-loved twosome known as Flanagan and Allen, famous for hit songs like 'Underneath the Arches', 'Hometown' and quite a few more. Bud had such an infectious smile and with his big, round mischievous eyes could act the innocent to great effect.

His weakness was betting on the horses – he was always a loser. To keep his habit going he decided that instead of losing money as a punter he'd become a bookmaker. He went into business with an astute boxing promoter named Jack Solomons. For a while he did okay, but the horses and the tax man soon caught up with him. Poor old Bud struggled to make ends meet, and he had to work hard until the day he died.

This lovable character once asked me to have lunch with him at Isows Jewish restaurant in Soho. When it came to paying the bill he said, 'I'll toss you who pays.' He spun a coin, I called 'heads' and he lost. Bud then asked me if I could hang on until 2.30 because he had a bet on a horse in the 2.20 at Newmarket. Well, it lost, so I paid the bill. That same evening, when I arrived at my dressing room, there was a bottle of Dom Perignon champagne in a bucket of ice, with a card saying 'Warm regards, Bud'.

*

The very first Royal Command Performance I was selected for was staged at the Palladium on 13 November 1950. There were some world-class acts appearing, and the stars in my eyes dazzled: Max Miller, Gracie Fields, singer Allan Jones of 'Donkey Serenade' fame, Tommy Trinder, Billy Cotton and his band, Jack Benny, Dinah Shore, Donald Peers, Max Wall, and Flanagan and Allen. There were some twenty others too, all top-line acts. But the star of stars on that occasion was King George's wife, later affectionately called the Queen Mother.

Everybody who met the Queen Mother had a story to tell of her warmth, her smile, her concern and the love she wanted to share. In my lifetime very few people have occasioned so much grief when the Reaper called. Outside my own immediate family, only Winston Churchill and Princess Diana come to mind.

Fifty-two years ago, I was honoured to perform for Her Majesty and King George VI for the first time. I sometimes get asked, was I nervous! Nervous? My knees were knocking. But compared to some of the experienced stalwarts from show business, I was relatively calm. My strongest memory of that night was at the beginning, just after the roll on the drums had been sounded. All was quiet for a second or two, and then Gracie Fields was supposed to sing unaccompanied the first four bars of the National Anthem – not an easy thing to do without a guide note of some kind.

Gracie sang 'God save our gracious King, long live our noble King . . .' It was then that the pit orchestra joined in, followed closely by the audience. Well, it should have been fine, but it wasn't. Gracie had pitched the song in her own key. The thirty-piece orchestra, conducted by Woolf Phillips, had to play what was written on their scores, which was in a different key. Some of the audience sang in Gracie's key, others with the orchestra. The artistes on stage tried to help our Gracie, but . . . It was chaotic. 'You have

73

never heard "God save the King" sung in six different keys before, have you?' remarked bandleader Billy Cotton afterwards, laughing fit to choke.

I was standing next to Gracie Fields in the middle of all this on stage. When Bud Flanagan led the three cheers for Their Majesties, over the 'hip, hip hoorays!' Gracie said to me, out of the corner of her mouth in her rich Lancashire accent, 'Hey lad, I really boogered that up, didn't I?'

I wasn't in the line-up to shake hands with Their Majesties – only about half a dozen of the big stars were allowed that privilege – but impressario Val Parnell was there. He later told me that when apologising to the Queen for the mix up of that 'most sacred of anthems', she said she thought it had been planned that way, and that she was highly amused.

Jack Benny was also on that star-studded programme. Oh what a nervous man. I had thought Frankie Howerd was the most nervous performer I'd ever met, but Jack, who became a lifelong friend, came a close second.

His fame had spread to these shores, and the British public was well aware that his stinginess was just an act. Everybody knew the routine where a hold-up man stuck a gun in Jack's ribs, saying, 'Your money or your life.' There was no response from Jack, so the mugger impatiently repeated, 'Your money or your life.' One of the biggest audience laughs ever heard was when Jack said, 'I'm thinking.' What a comedian. I learned so much from him years later when he invited me over to Hollywood to appear on three of his TV shows.

*

My next Royal line-up was again at the London Palladium. It took place on 3 November 1952, and there were artistes galore, including Arthur Askey, the Beverley Sisters, Reg Dixon, Beniamino Gigli, Jewel and Warriss, Vic Oliver, Norman Wisdom, Ted Ray, Winifred Atwell, Eve Boswell, Gracie Fields, Tony Hancock, Vera Lynn, Terry Thomas,

The Tiller Girls and Maurice Chevalier, plus at least thirty other names from the field of variety.

Tony Hancock, who had been a sidekick in the *Educating Archie* radio show, was making a great impact, not only on *Archie* but on his own as the out-of-work actor 'know all'. His catchphrase 'flippin kids' was enjoyed by parents everywhere, and he was to go from strength to strength. Winifred Atwell seemed to be on the radio every time you switched on, and the warm and likeable northern comedian Reg Dixon had had a big hit with his song 'Confidentially'.

The most unhappy man on that 1952 list of performers was Gigli, at the time reckoned to be the world's greatest tenor. It seemed he had nowhere to practise while waiting to sing. I kept bumping into him in corridors, dressing rooms, on stage, off stage. I knew only two words of Italian then, and he knew only two words of English. Gracie Fields was of some help as she had gone to live on the Isle of Capri and had recently married an Italian, a tradesman who had come to repair her 'wireless'. To Gigli she would cheerfully say *'Bon giorno,* Beniamino'. I don't know what he made of Gracie's Italian spoken with a Lancashire accent, but he always replied with the only two words of English he had learned: 'Winston Churchill'. It was the only time I ever saw him smile.

Ted Ray, one of my favourite comedians on and off stage, was a great ad lib comic. One morning during a coffee break he tried to explain that the BBC TV director Albert Stevenson was a great sentimentalist. When I asked Ted why he thought Arthur was so, he told me, 'He goes to the cinema and cries at trailers.' This really amused me. For the next couple of years Ted would send me postcards from different places with a play on the same words. I can't remember all of them, but one postcard was from Cornwall telling me that he had been booked to appear at a caravan park in that neck of the woods. He went on to say that during his performance there was a big fire. Many of the caravans had caught fire and the owners were naturally very upset – all this to tell me he had never witnessed 'so many crying at trailers'.

Jewel and Warriss were 'big time' at this stage of their career. I didn't know much about Jimmy Jewel, but Ben Warriss was a dapper, stylish dresser who wore custom-made suits and shoes. He had taken to smoking with a large cigarette holder and did the round of London's nightclubs with his dog on a lead. He was a generous tipper and was welcomed by the waiters and management at the best restaurants.

We were to meet a few months later in New York, when I was working at the Palace theatre. Jewel and Warriss flew in for a one-night stand on the renowned Ed Sullivan television show. We were all staying at the Park Sheraton Hotel, which overlooked Central Park.

This was at the time when a Mafia godfather named Anastasia had been shot while sitting in a barber's chair. The bellboy who told us the story added, 'He died last night.' Ben piped up, 'He wasn't the only one who died last night – we both died on the Ed Sullivan show.' They did too. One write-up said that they tried to be too much like Abbott and Costello. This really annoyed Ben and Jimmy because they had been performing long before Abbott and Costello had even met.

Also on that Palladium bill were the very young and professional Beverley Sisters, dressed alike. They must have been doing something right because they are still going strong and still 'wowing 'em'.

*

The following year I was selected yet again for the Royal Command Performance to be staged 2 November, this time at the London Coliseum. King George VI had passed away and we had a new young queen. There were concerns that some of the older comics might chance a risqué line, so the censorship on comedy was very strict.

I enjoyed being chosen for 'Commands'. It was a great chance to meet old friends and make new ones. In that 1953 line-up star names included Henry Cotton, Jimmy James, the John Tiller Girls, Dick James, Ronnie Ronalde and Pearl Carr.

We were all a bit wary of Eamonn Andrews because he had started a show called *This is Your Life*. None of us knew if the red book would be presented to one of us with the words 'this is your life', but nobody was caught.

Dick James was a band singer, very pally, a joy to be with. He always had a new joke and always wore a smile, even though life for him at the time was a bit of a struggle. Then he founded a music company that held the copyrights of a particular group of singers, which made him a very, very, very wealthy man. The singers were, of course, The Beatles. Big money!

*

In 1954 I was included in the line-up once again, my fourth 'Command' in four years. I had done more Royal Shows than Her Majesty! That year there were quite a few new faces as well as old friends: Frankie Lane, Bob Hope, Arthur Askey, Eddie Calvert, Thora Hird, Al Read, Norman Wisdom, Richard Hearne, Ted Heath and his music, Howard Keel, Jack Parnell and Orchestra, Jack Buchanan, Noel Coward, Guy Mitchell, Peter Sellers, Dickie Valentine, Gracie Fields and some thirty other 'bill-toppers'.

During that year I had been having success in the record industry, with songs like 'Tulips from Amsterdam', 'You Need Hands', 'Out of Town' and, would you believe, 'You're a Pink Toothbrush'. If you look at the music of that last song you'll find it took four experienced music men to write it, one of them the aforementioned Dick James. It still gets a huge amount of requests.

One of my most successful records, which stayed in the Top Twenty for sixteen weeks, was a burlesque of all the Frankie Laine hits, called 'The Cowpuncher's Cantata'. I had never met Frankie Laine and when I discovered we were on the bill together for this RCP I was a little concerned about how he had taken my 'send up'. When we were introduced, I found that he had thankfully never heard of me, which saved a lot of explaining. He had hit after hit – when I introduced him to the audience I told them, 'Frankie Laine is almost never out of the hit parade. When he was once, a month ago, he complained to his doctor of a slipped disc.'

Another singer I introduced on that 1954 show was Guy Mitchell. He was very popular here in England, although not everybody had heard of him. A director friend named Charles Reading told me of a day he was at rehearsals and Val Parnell confessed he had run out of stars to top the bill at the Palladium. Charles suggested Guy Mitchell. 'Guy who?' Parnell confessed he had never heard of him and asked what he did.

Charles told Parnell just to watch and then walked over to the sixteen Tiller Girls, who were having a short break from rehearsals. He got their attention, then asked, 'Girls, have you ever heard of Guy Mitchell?' There was a scream from them and then they began to sing lines from 'There's a Pawnshop on the Corner' followed by 'Truly Truly Fair' and then 'She Wears Red Feathers'. Val Parnell booked Guy Mitchell and sold out at every performance.

*

After all the Royal shows in the fifties I became a 'regular' at the Palladium. The shows featured some of the best acts in the world. The bills always included what were called 'speciality' acts, usually non-speaking performers, plus jugglers, slack-wire balancing acts and acrobats. It was Val Parnell's firm belief that no audience could concentrate on more than twelve minutes of patter without music from the pit orchestra assuring everybody it was still breathing. That's why a variety bill usually had seven or eight 'speciality' acts.

*

The 1955 Royal Command Performance was held on 7 November at the Victoria Palace, which is a short walk from Buckingham Palace. This was after there had been a Royal attendance in April at the Opera House in Blackpool, featuring many well-known stars from the north. Reginald Dixon, Morecambe and Wise, Bill Waddington, Arthur Askey, the Littlewood Girls Choir, Wilfred Pickles, Albert Modley and Al Read were among the international bill. It was one of the very few shows produced outside of London.

At the Victoria Palace, popular performers like Dave King, Benny Hill, Lena Horne, Ruby Murray and Johnnie Ray gave their services for 'another one-night stand'.

*

When I was looking over the list of artistes taking part in the 1960 Royal Command Performance, which was at the Victoria Palace on 16 May, I could not remember where they dressed or rehearsed. It is the longest list of performers ever assembled. I remember vividly some names, but others I have no idea what they did – does anybody remember Charles Yawns?

I do recall Diana Dors with her then husband Dickie Dawson. I had spent some time with them at their home in Hollywood. When they divorced Dickie made a name for himself as a quiz master on American TV, then later did well in movies and actually became more famous in the States than Diana.

Another star on the bill was the bundle of energy named Sammy Davis Jnr. And also Nat King Cole. I had to introduce him. I walked to a dark corner of the stage to wait for the preceding act to finish, and saw a red glow that I almost walked into. Just in time the lights came on and I saw that the glow I had almost bumped into was the end of a cigarette in a long holder being puffed by Nat King Cole. He was having a crafty smoke before he did his act. He told me the holder was a special one to filter out nicotine, but it didn't help – Nat died later of throat cancer.

Lonnie Donegan was never out of the hit parade with his skiffle. Jimmy Edwards was still being censored. There were also two great vocalists, one of whom, Dickie Valentine, was later tragically killed in an awful automobile accident. The other, still with us and doing a great job on radio, is Ronnie Hilton. Liberace was invited again, to make up for his cancellation in 1956, and was a big, big success.

Cliff Richard and the Shadows made their debut on that particular Royal Command Performance, which means he has been around for more than forty years as a top o' the bill. That's some achievement for a pop singer. Another achiever who was consolidating his future, not only as a quiz master but also as an entertainer supreme, was Bruce Forsyth. He has managed to stay at the top on sheer talent and 'know how' ever since he appeared on *Sunday Night at the London Palladium*, asking contestants to beat the clock.

Adam Faith was another new kid on the block, who later surprised a few with his acting ability and writing a weekly column on finance for stockholders. His brain is too fertile to rest on laurels, and I wouldn't be in the least surprised if Adam doesn't turn up in some other sphere – maybe as Prime Minister!

But seriously, folks, let me tell you about Hughie Green. *Opportunity Knocks* was the number one show on television. Hughie was in charge and enjoying every moment of his deserved success. During the rehearsals for the Royal Command Performance, Hughie, who was a qualified pilot, approached me to appear in a benefit show he was doing for the RAF Benevolent Fund. Unfortunately he had picked a date when I would be in Spain and couldn't make the journey. 'I'll fly down and pick you up, then fly you back to Spain next day,' he said. I told him that with the greatest will in the world it would be impossible. He raised that famous eyebrow and said, 'Look, this is for those guys who risked their lives for us.' I replied, 'I know Hughie – I was one of them.'

For the next two years at Thames Television, where we both recorded our TV shows, Hughie would ignore me, in the canteen, in the bar, on the set. He had made up his mind never to speak to me again.

One winter, I was in Barbados and drove out from the city with my wife to see the set that had been built for the Harry Belafonte movie *Island in the Sun*. The place was deserted except for a black security man. As we made our way around the replica of the mansion, I turned a corner and there with movie camera coming towards me was Hughie Green. 'Hello', I said, 'aren't you Harry Belafonte?' Hughie introduced his lady, then invited us back to his hotel for drinks. We accepted, and it was as if there had never been a rift between us. He raised his glass and toasted me, 'Cheers to a dear old friend.' I replied, 'I'll drink to that.' The ladies said 'Good health' and then raised their Campari sodas. I repeat, 'That's show business.'

The list on that bill also included some of Britain's top funny men. There was my old friend Frankie Howerd, who was 'red hot', as well as Bob Monkhouse, Norman Wisdom, Charlie Drake, Jimmy Edwards, Bruce Forsyth, Benny Hill, Alfred Marks, The Lynton Boys, and Harry Worth and the Crazy Gang. All of us were vying for the biggest laugh of the night, a line quoted by the press next day with a picture or two.

It's strange, but the only joke I can remember from that show was one cracked by Harry Worth. He said he went to his local grocery shop to buy a bottle of sauce, and the grocer said, 'Would you like HP?' Harry replied, 'No thank you. I'll pay cash.' Such a simple line, but it got one of the biggest laughs of the night. I think it was because the audience were aware that the Royal party would not have had any idea what HP meant, that very few of them knew it stood for 'hire purchase'. Very little of that goes on among crowned heads.

*

The list for the Royal Command show at the Prince of Wales Theatre on 6 November 1961 contained some really good performers. Many previous RCPs had names that were unable to 'do an act', so they would be used to 'dress' the stage or do a 'walk on' to introduce another act. It made for good box office and filled the programmes that were on sale for £5 each in aid of the benevolent fund to keep the costly Brinsworth House, a home for aged entertainers, solvent.

Many of the names on this bill were featured in a long-running show I was heading at the Prince of Wales Theatre, called *Do-Re-Mi*. It was a tough show for me because I was on stage for the whole of the two hours, except for the interval. I had dialogue that had to be performed in an American accent to play the part of Hubie Cramm. And I had an actress playing opposite me as my wife whom I had to match for energy. This was Maggie Fitzgibbons, an Australian actress who was among the finest leading ladies on the London stage. We played eight shows a week that included two afternoon matinees. I was certainly happy to get to bed after driving back to my home at Leatherhead after the curtain fell.

It was so different from my solo act, which I could revamp by putting new material in or taking it out. The lines learned for *Do-Re-Mi* had to be strictly adhered to because other actors on stage were taking cues from me. I haven't mentioned this before, but I was not sorry when the show closed after eight months.

For the RCP that year I had no need to rehearse any new ideas. We just slotted a scene from *Do-Re-Mi* into the spot selected. No worries.

It gave me the chance to meet some names I had never met before. Acker Bilk, with whom I later made a CD album, was one. We had one of the happiest weeks I have ever spent in a studio, and we remain good friends.

Many years later I was in New Zealand. I woke around

5 a.m. and, as the hotel was on the beach and the beach was deserted, I decided to stroll along the golden sands. I walked quite a way and then, in the far distance, I saw another lonely figure tossing pebbles into the quiet Pacific. As we got nearer to each other, I couldn't believe it, the stranger on the shore was Acker Bilk – neither of us knew the other was in New Zealand.

Nina and Frederick were a big attraction in those days. They were a handsome couple with Nordic accents that suited their style of play. They later divorced but at the time they were portrayed as the devoted couple. Nina had a face the TV cameras loved to get close to. Frederick had a serenity that seemed to say, 'I am with one of the world's most beautiful women.' They were adored by most of the British public who took them to their hearts.

At a later date, when I was using guest artistes on my TV show, we booked Nina who had broken up with Frederick and gone solo. She arrived at the rehearsal rooms with a hacking cough that made her shudder right down to her ankles. She wore no make up and sniffed like a bull. She had no idea what to sing, so we started sorting out ideas. And then she went into a huddle with the wardrobe mistress, trying to find a creation to cover her beautiful form. Each suggestion was 'no-noed'. The designer clothes, which didn't come cheap, caused a wrinkling of that beautiful nose and a shake of the head. This was using up a lot of precious rehearsal time.

Then I had an idea. I told Nina that when I worked with Judy Garland in the US, one of the most memorable moments was when Judy went off stage wearing an elegant dress and then, after a quick change, came back on in a tramp's outfit to perform 'We're a Couple of Swells'. Nina went for that. So dressed as tramps, faces dabbed with soot, we performed 'I live in Trafalgar Square', which is about a couple of tramps sleeping on the benches. It was very effective, we got fantastic applause and the wardrobe department saved a fortune by using the tramp outfits. I don't know where Nina is nowadays, or Frederick, but I hope they are both happy and healthy.

Lovely Jack Benny and adorable George Burns were performing on that bill too, George with more stories about his vaudeville days and Jack helpless with laughter. Jack Benny had brought his wife Mary over from LA. She was assertive but always in Jack's interest.

I remember once during the sixties I was invited to appear on *The Jack Benny Show* in California. For most of the time I was there I used to have dinner with Jack, his wife Mary and several show-business friends at his house in Beverly Hills.

After dinner one night, Mary put her coat on to take their poodle for a walk round the block before retiring. Jack and I sat in the lounge armchairs, puffing contentedly on our Havana cigars.

The film star James Stewart lived on the same block as Jack. He had recently made a movie called *The Glenn Miller Story*. He liked the idea of the rimless spectacles he used in the film and after the filming he took to wearing them regularly. Almost every impressionist in America at that time was impersonating James Stewart. It was an easy impression – all one had to do was fish a pair of rimless glasses out of a pocket and drawl: 'Well – er – just a minute – er – hold on . . .' Thunderous applause as it was so recognisable!

The drawl became a trademark.

When Mary arrived back at the house with the poodle she said to Jack, 'I just met Jimmy Stewart on the block. He was walking his dog. I said, "How are you, Jimmy?" And you'd have thought he was doing an impression of himself when he said [Mary went into an impression], "Waal – er – look – er – Mary – I – er – er . . ." I could stand it no longer, so I said: "Look Jimmy, it's chilly. I don't want an impersonation, I just want to know how you are!"' With that, she told Jack, she walked off.

Jack was flabbergasted. He clapped his hands to his face, which was a familiar gesture on his shows, and said in disbelief, 'Oh Mary, you didn't say that to Jimmy?'

The dog began to bark. Mary looked at her husband and said, 'You can cut out your impersonation of Jack Benny, and *you* [pointing at the dog], you can stop your impression of Ethel Merman!'

INTERVAL CHAT

How the Palladium became the world's most famous theatre is a mystery to many. Situated in a side street off Oxford Street, it has a small entrance and many do not know how to pronounce the name of the street it is in (Argyle Street). They are aware of the next turning – Carnaby Street – made famous by The Beatles in the sixties, but for years as a theatre it was too far off the map for regular theatre-goers to bother with. They enjoyed the square mile around Shaftesbury Avenue.

As a teenager my most vivid memory of the dozens of times I stood looking at the photographs outside the Palladium was of a short-sleeved commissionaire polishing the thick brass banister that led up to the entrance of the Stalls and the Upper Circle. This was usually in the morning. The street was busy with delivery men for the cafés, especially the Lyons Corner House at the bottom left-hand corner. Then came the war!

One of the turning points for the Palladium was when the managing director, George Black, thought up the idea of bringing comedians together and calling them The Crazy Gang. They were Flanagan and Allen, Nervo and Knox, and

Naughton and Gold, each of them a fully experienced double act. In no time their fame spread, they became a great draw and the theatre was on its way to having a big money-spinner. The box office cash registers never stopped ringing.

The first time I ever entered the building was as an A/C II in the RAF. I was home on leave. Adolf Hitler had been knocking London about with the Luftwaffe, but on a quiet day with not an air-raid siren to be heard I found my way to Oxford Circus. I queued up to pay my one and sixpence for a seat in the Circle, to watch Max Miller and Vera Lynn plus some wonderful supporting acts, and sixteen of the prettiest chorus girls, in a revue titled *Applesauce*.

The reason I was there was mostly because of a pal in the RAF with whom I sometimes did a double act. His name was Roger Welch. He had told me his sister was co-starring with Max Miller. I scanned my programme looking for Vera Welch, but she wasn't there. It wasn't until well into the programme, when the stage lit up and, draped in a magic blue focus a girl singer appeared – shy but friendly, with a voice that went out to every patron – that I realised Vera *Lynn* was Roger's sister. She had changed her name from Welch to Lynn. I wanted to turn round to announce, 'I know her brother', but I kept 'schtoom'.

Peace came, and after a while the Palladium went back to being the white elephant it had been pre-war. In the meantime, George Black had died, and the impressario's crown was taken over by Val Parnell, a massive man who stood six feet three inches. He oozed power. Very few people argued with him. We became the best of pals. There was a great difference in our ages, but for many years he and his wife, a lovely Hawaiian lady named Helen, were like close relatives.

Val Parnell had the idea of importing American top-liners to the theatre for two-week engagements. His first signing was one of the world's greatest and best-known movie stars, Mickey Rooney. He was a disaster – crucified by the British press.

It wasn't entirely poor Mickey's fault. He had been the number-one movie star in the universe, even surpassing the box-office appeal of the great Clark Gable, who had won every accolade Hollywood could think of with his portrayal of Rhett Butler in the classic film, *Gone with the Wind*.

The bookers had seen Mickey do 'Let's do the show right here!', with the likes of Judy Garland and other leading ladies who were the best in Glitterland. But movies are a lot different to being on a stage, alone, in a spotlight, with no retakes. Reputations don't matter – you are paid to entertain, and Mickey wasn't experienced enough to pull it off. It's different being the canopy name in an American nightclub, with a half-sozzled audience. There all you do is walk around shaking hands with ringsiders, saying, 'Hi. My name's Mickey Rooney. What's yours?' When you have done the handshaking and the half dozen jokes, you finish on a light song and get off. It's money for jam. But British audiences, brought up in variety theatres, were used to seeing good disciplined acts that knew their 'patter'. They were and are a lot more discerning.

On that Palladium bill, a northern comedian named Jimmy James was a supporting act for Rooney. He stole the show. The critics liked his style. He got a much kinder press and it started Jimmy James on a new career.

Don't get me wrong – I would never malign another performer. Mickey Rooney did come back – he found some good movies to get him out of that transitional period when he was too old to play the teenager he had portrayed in the Andy Hardy films, but too young and too short to play leading men. When he was an 'in-between' he was in dire straits with the American tax officers, and his marriages had left him penniless. At one time he owned six racehorses . . . 'I gave most of my money to sick animals. Mind, I didn't know they were sick before the race!' he often cracked.

He got booked into a revue in the seventies called *Sugar Babies*. It ran in New York and toured America for six years.

It came to London, and opened at the Savoy Theatre. I went backstage to say how much I had enjoyed it. He asked me to have a cup of tea and sit down for a chat, which I did. Then for the next three hours we talked about his heyday, his career and his marriages. He told me he'd lost count of his grandchildren.

Now he's back on the road and making a go of it with his present wife (number seven). He makes a decent living and people still love to shake his hand. The one topic he doesn't like to be reminded of is his appearance at the London Palladium. 'I just wasn't ready,' he says.

The last picture I have of him was that night in his dressing room at the Savoy Theatre. I looked up to see him gently nodding off to sleep. I let myself out quietly, and told the stagedoor keeper that Mr Rooney was asleep. He nodded knowingly. I left by the Exit door.

STARS, UNDER PARS AND CARS

From the fifties on, the place to meet the established 'stars' was on a golf course. Bob Hope and Bing Crosby were among the first to popularise this sport. Until then the general feeling was that the game was only for presidents, royalty or bank managers. The rules were strict, too strict for the peasants to obey, or so the ordinary man was led to believe.

But, bit by bit, players who had been ball boys, caddies or locker-room attendants found themselves allowed to hit a few balls down at the range, and found too that they became proficient at the game. Suddenly, golf club secretaries and people in charge were allowing the workers to represent their club if they showed promise.

This is what happened to some of the 'greats' playing nowadays. They couldn't afford the game of golf as workers, but were spurred on by the talent they knew they had. Tony Jacklin, Peter Allis, Seve Ballesteros and Australian Greg Norman are a few of the golf stars it has been my privilege to partner or play against. Each of them came up the hard way. I have spent many happy hours in their company listening to their stories of trials and tribulations on their way to the top.

I was at Moor Park several years ago, waiting for Greg Norman to tee off. He swung and we watched in awe as the ball sailed more than three hundred yards down the fairway. I shook my head, saying to Greg, 'I wish I could hit a ball like that.' Greg replied, 'I wish I could tell a joke like you.' I guess that sums it up. We all have to find our own way.

A moment that impressed me about him was when I was in a golf club at Southport in Queensland, Australia. The member I was playing with left to say hello to Greg Norman's mother. 'How is Greg?' I heard him ask her as we made our way down the fairway. Her answer was: 'I'll give him Greg when I see him – three bloody weeks and not even a postcard.' Greg had been competing in Hong Kong and Japan, and I suppose the last thing on this young fellow's mind was a postcard to his mum.

Another favourite memory was sometime later, at the air terminal in Hong Kong. Greg could not get on a fully booked British Airways flight (BOAC then) to London. I went over to the English girl on the desk, who recognised me from TV, and told her that if this tall, blonde handsome cowboy did not get on the plane to London he would lose the part he was auditioning for – as the new James Bond. She was impressed! Not only was a seat found, but he was upgraded to first class. To this day I don't think he knows that I was the one who pulled the strings.

Another 'star', England's greatest golfer at that time, was Tony Jacklin. We were playing a very slow game in the Bing Crosby Open at Gleneagles in Scotland. During the wait, Tony started singing softly to himself. I asked him if he had ever done any crooning and he laughed, saying 'Come on.' Several weeks later, there was a spot in my television show for a golfer to sing a couple of choruses with lyrics about golfing. It had to be performed as a Gilbert and Sullivan piece.

I remembered Tony's very nice rendering on the golf course, so called him on the phone and proposed the piece to be sung. At first he was most reluctant, but I persuaded him to come and take the part in my show the following week. He was a sensation! I told him afterwards that if he ever gave up golf he could always get a booking with the D'Oyly Carte. So far he hasn't bothered. Tony is one of golf's true gentlemen.

*

Because theatrical players are usually free during the day, working only at night, many have taken up the game and become quite good at it. Let me tell you a story about my friend Jimmy Tarbuck.

Jimmy is a good comedian. When he is 'on form', there are very few patter comics who can equal his delivery and cheek. He doesn't always make friends because he usually goes for the laugh, regardless of the embarrassment his jokes can sometimes bring. But he doesn't do it deliberately to hurt. It's just that he can't resist the sound that is music to any comedian's ears – the sound of laughter.

On a couple of occasions I have had to let him know that I wasn't all that pleased about some gibe he had made about me. I take a lot of stick from impersonators that, at times, gets a bit personal, and Jimmy in the past has hit below the belt . . . But I like him and regard him as a friend. His heart is in the right place and I can assure you he wouldn't hurt you intentionally.

A few years ago, he was in a summer show at Bournemouth. I am a resident of Bournemouth so we met regularly at Parkstone Golf Club for a game. He is a far better golfer than I could ever hope to be. He gave me a generous stroke advantage and we'd play for a couple of golf balls. Almost every time he'd win, and I had to forfeit two new golf balls.

At the time Jim had lost his driving licence for speeding and had to use a driver, who also caddied for him. One day we had played as usual, Jim had won and, as usual, I had to pay with two new golf balls. As I passed his Rolls in the car park, his driver was putting Jim's clubs in the boot. I noticed there was a box of new balls. With a wink to the driver, I took two new balls, unseen by Jim, then walked to the front of the car and gave him his own golf balls with, 'H'y'are, Jim – what I owe you.' He took the balls, gave them to the driver to put in the boot of the car, said 'Cheerio' and went off.

The next time we met, I did the same thing, and kept it going for half a dozen games. Eventually, I took the whole box of twelve balls and, on this particular day, said, 'Here, Jim, you played so well today, I want to give you a box of a dozen balls.' He took them and walked to the boot to put them in with his clubs. It was obvious he was missing something. He turned to see the driver and me grinning from ear to ear. He looked at the balls, realised they were his own and with three words summed me up: 'You conniving bastard!'

Jim tells this story quite often. I hope he adds that I did give him a legitimate extra dozen balls as compensation.

*

I have often said that if you play a man three rounds of golf you'll find the man's true nature: whether he's polite, a cheat, single-minded, good fun. Almost every quality comes to the surface, and after eighteen holes you will know your partner pretty well.

I have played several times with Sean Connery, seen his eyes blaze at a bad shot, seen him get short-tempered at being held up by a slow game ahead and listened to him wax lyrical about his childhood days in Edinburgh. He's a good bloke.

Today he is a fine amateur golfer, but this story took place when he was like most of us beginners – bloody awful!

It was at Coombe Hill Golf Club just outside London. Eric Sykes and I took on Sean and actor Stanley Baker, later knighted. We beat them hands down. Afterwards in the club house Sean came up and placed £60 on the counter with, 'Here y'are, Max. You'll find that correct.' I asked Sean what the money was for. He explained we had a £20 bet on the first nine holes, £20 on the second and £20 on the game. 'That's £60,' he smiled.

I was puzzled by this – I had never played for this amount. The most I ever wagered was a couple of quid on a game. As Sean walked away Eric Sykes entered. I told him that Sean had just paid me £60. That's a couple of hundred quid by today's standard.

Eric told me that Stanley Baker had just paid him the same amount. 'Did you make a bet?' I asked Eric. He confessed that Sean had mumbled something in his Scottish accent and Eric, whose hearing is impaired, just nodded his head, so Sean must have assumed we had a bet on.

As Eric and I drank our drinks our eyes met and we began to laugh – laugh hysterically – because we were both thinking the same thing: 'What a fight there would have been if we'd lost!'

*

Eric Sykes and I have been pals for more than forty years. If he or I ever needed a friend, I think we would call on each other first. Eric is a very fine scriptwriter and a very funny man. He discovered his comedy talent when we were both signed for the BBC radio show *Educating Archie*.

When we were first given the scripts – usually on Sunday morning to be performed 'live' Sunday evening – we'd read our parts in flat early-morning voices. It was the inflection of the delivery that brought Eric's scripts to life. That was how Hancock's 'flippin kids' was born, and how I made a national catch phrase of 'A good idea, son!'

It was because of our uninspired early-morning reading that Eric decided to read out his own comedy lines. It ended up being half an hour of hilarity as he played each part himself. He managed to give us laughs that were unseen on a first reading, and as a result we all knew how to attack the script.

From this his confidence grew. When the series came to an end he entered the film world. His silent movies – *The Plank* among others – plus his long-running television series with Hattie Jacques, endeared him to audiences worldwide.

Eric and I became keen golfers together and are now quite competent players, but in the early days we were like most others that take up the game – hackers!

It was during these 'hacking' days that Eric bought a house for his growing family. He had married a lovely lady who was his nurse when he suffered ear trouble and was hospitalised in London. Edith nursed him then and has looked after him since. They have four super children. I am godfather to one of them.

About the time I am talking about, the mid fifties, it was reported that I was the highest paid performer in Great Britain. I was almost resident comedian at the London Palladium, on radio every week and on television, with best-selling records. My name was on billboards all over London. (I have to tell you this because I thought it would have been impossible to have been British and not know the name of Max Bygraves.)

Back to the 'hacking' . . . It was Eric's greatest wish to become a member of the St George's Hill Golf Club – his home backed onto the third hole, and it would have been so convenient. So he had made an application to join.

On this particular day, we were out on the course, having paid our fees and got permission to play. As we searched for a lost ball on the fourth hole, two golf balls landed quite near us, without us hearing a 'Fore!', 'Look out', or 'Kiss my foot!' Soon after, two irate red-faced 'gentlemen' – and I use the word loosely – humphed their way past, bristling with anger. Later on many more golfers came through. Eric and I thought that was all part of golf etiquette, and we went on looking for our balls. We were that inexperienced. A couple of days later, Eric received a letter from the club secretary. I can't remember it word for word, but in essence it read:

> Dear Mr Sykes,
> You interrupted a competition on this course today – no courtesy was extended to the competitors and your manners leave a lot to be desired.
>   We understand you are desirous of becoming a member of this club; if this is the behaviour we are to expect, we beg you not to bother. This applies to your partner Max Hargreaves also.
> Yours etc.

All this happened more than 45 years ago. Eric, who still lives nearby, enjoys golf but is still not a member.

*

CARS

The first car I was able to afford was a Ford Anglia. I bought it at a showroom right next door to the Metropolitan Theatre in the Edgware Road, London, where I was appearing each night for a week. As I entered the stage door, this all black, shiny four-seater with number plate GUF 650 seemed to beckon to me from the centre of the showroom. It was priced at £450, which in 1948 was a lotta money to somebody like myself.

Topping the bill at the Met that week was an act called The Nitwits, a very funny musical act made up of six very accomplished musicians who were trying something different and being very successful. The vocalist and guitarist was Ronnie Genarder, a Scot with a most likeable manner.

We had become good friends. Midweek Ronnie arrived at the stage door to see me gazing at 'Guff' (as I had christened the four-seater). 'Thinking of buying it?' he asked. I told him what I had been telling myself all week, that I couldn't afford it.

'Of course you can afford it.' He then began to plan my career for me. 'You'll have to travel, and you'll need it for dates up and down the country. You've got a wife and two kids – you'll have more – you're young . . .' I argued that I had no garage because I had no home, and that I didn't have a licence to drive a car – I had driven RAF trucks now and again but I . . . Ronnie stopped me. 'I'll teach you to drive.'

By the end of the week I was the owner of Guff, which almost left me broke. The following week Ronnie was giving me driving lessons and proved to be a superb teacher. Soon after I was able to take a test and remove the 'L' plates.

Nothing can match the thrill of owning your first car. Oh the loving care and spit and polish bestowed on Guff. I was the owner of the only car in the long street we were living in at Romford. Cars were rarer in those days than they are now – you'd be surprised how many more friends you made when you owned one. Children would stop to admire the dream machine that did 40 miles to the gallon and could reach 60 miles per hour in one minute from start. I was so proud.

With a new car I also had a new agent – Jock Jacobsen, who began to book me on quality dates. These were bookings I could take now because I was mobile. Journeys could be mapped out easily, and there were no traffic jams like nowadays. But take it from me, there is no truth when people tell you the world was different then and people were more caring.

One morning I went out on the street and started to work on Guff with my chamois leather, and almost cried. Some fiend had made a series of criss-crosses with a sharp nail across the bonnet. I couldn't believe it. What had I done to deserve this? I hardly knew anybody in the street and they hardly knew me. I always believed I was modest, not given to airs, liked to help others etc. Then a hint was dropped by a neighbour that perhaps it was because I was Jewish.

'But I'm Catholic', I told them. They were not convinced. 'Max is a Jewish name,' said somebody. That's what it was all about. Somebody believed me to be Jewish and for no other reason had decided to run a nail over the car. This was in 1948 when the war was over, Hitler had been exterminated and the world was supposedly a better place. Along with millions of others, I had been in uniform for four years and thought I had done a decent job. And now, on the outskirts of Romford, Essex, I had been singled out for some hatred.

If you think *that* was hurtful, you should have heard some of the remarks when I went places in my first Rolls Royce. Afterwards, I toughened up and thought 'they can think what they like'. My granddad had been a currier of leather at Connolly's, who supplied the upholstery for Rolls Royces – sweated labour you wouldn't think existed in pre-war Britain. It was with his help to his daughter – my mother – that we got by. So, I have only one word for those ignorant racist ba. . ...ds and it isn't 'mazel -tov'!

The vandalism to Guff made me remember another incident when I was a serving aircraftsman in the RAF. I hadn't attached much importance to it at the time. It was during my training days, when a crowd of us were sitting around a pot-bellied stove trying to keep warm. It was night time and a discussion had begun about the terrible time the Jews in Germany were suffering.

Somebody mentioned 'gefilte' fish, and somebody else asked what 'gefilte' was. Another said, 'Ask Max. He'll know – he's Jewish.' I told them I couldn't help as I was very English and very Catholic. To convince them, I sang part of the mass in Latin. Then I told them the answers I gave the priest when serving mass while swinging the burning incense. The silence was broken by some joker we called Rasher who said, 'Now show us your d..k.'

*

After I had knocked up some 30,000 miles in the Anglia I sold it to a midget from an act known as the Pirates for £200.

He put blocks on the pedals and ran it for another 30,000 miles, then sold it for £250. That was after he'd put a reconditioned engine in, which set him back £38. I wonder how it finished its life – I really loved old Guff.

My next car was an Armstrong Siddeley, a much larger saloon-type car, JUC 595. It was almost new, 8,000 miles on the clock and cost £1,000. I adored it in a different way to Guff. There were quite a lot of teething troubles with 'Juck', as I had named it, so much so that I dreamed up a comedy routine that went along these lines . . . 'Just bought a new car. The salesman said it had belonged to a preacher. I think it must have been John the Baptist – every day I prayed it would start. When I went to road test it, I noticed two house bricks on the passenger seat. I threw them out the side window, and the salesman said, "There goes your handbrake." As I started to slowly move, the salesman's children were running excitedly alongside, shouting "It goes! It goes!" . . .' That routine got big laughs, so in a way Juck paid for itself.

I traded it in for a brand new Mark 7 Jaguar. I loved the Jag until one fateful Sunday morning, on a very wet rain-sodden trip from Nottingham to London for the recording of an *Educating Archie* episode, the Jag began to glide of its own free will! Luckily it was early in the morning and there were no other vehicles in sight. Doing a modest sixty I mounted a verge, went headlong into a ditch and finished up with two punctured tyres and a shattered windscreen. That was the only accident I had in all my years as a driver, and it was all thanks to an oil slick on the road. It could have been so much worse . . .

Even after I had the Jag fixed, it still wasn't right. That was when I met Billy Cotton, the bandleader.

He wasn't a great musician, but he could pick a 'sour' note out of a symphony orchestra. He had once been a footballer who was considered for the third division, and a racing car driver – he did all the things considered 'macho'.

When he took me into his London apartment, I couldn't believe the trophies on display. Up until then, I had thought of him as the bloke who wagged his finger in front of the band and shouted 'Wakey, Wakey'.

Bill loved to laugh, and he loved anybody who could make him laugh. In the early fifties I had tapped that laugh vein when we were billed together at the London Palladium in the show *Wonderful Time*. On a few occasions I almost made him choke with laughter.

One of those occasions was when we were on holiday together at Alassio in Italy. We'd gone to see the local football team play a team from San Remo. The small stadium was packed. I didn't speak too much Italian in those days, but the attitude of the locals was enough to tell me that most of their words would never be used in church. A bad decision by the referee brought a scene similar to mutiny, with bottles being thrown. Suddenly 'bang!', a lemonade bottle came hurtling from the back of the crowd and hit Billy full force on the shoulder. 'Jeeze,' shuddered Bill, after he'd got back some of his composure, 'if that lemonade bottle had been six inches higher, it could have killed me.' I made him laugh when I said, 'Good thing it was a soft drink!'

Bill was a popular customer with the Rolls Royce dealer Jack Barclay in Berkeley Square. One day he asked me to join him for lunch at his club, which was a few doors from Jack Barclay's. He introduced me to a French wine, which he enjoyed calling 'Nuts Saint George'. The French have a different pronunciation for it, but Bill liked to pretend he was an ignoramus. When the waiter pronounced 'Nuits' the right way, Bill just said, 'Yus, that's right mate – give us a pint of that.'

We left the club in a merry state, and as we passed the car showroom Bill stopped to look at the Rolls and Bentleys on offer. The star item was an almost new Rolls Royce, a 'Silver Dawn' in pristine condition with just under 2,000 miles on the clock. 'Why don't you treat yourself to that?' Bill asked me. I told him I couldn't afford it. He took my arm and steered me into the showroom where the salesman made a fuss of him. He asked the price of the 'Silver Dawn' and was told £4,500. 'It's not for me, it's for him,' he said, jerking his thumb at me.

To cut a long story short, Bill and three salesmen convinced me I needed that Rolls Royce. There and then I wrote the cheque, and was told they would deliver it to the London Palladium in two days. Just before the Wednesday matinee I was taken outside the stage door to see the Rolls Royce fitted with the personalised number plate MB 1. Bill told me the salesman must have gone to a lot of trouble to find this exclusive number plate and that it would be courteous to send him a case of whisky, which I did.

Forty-six years later I sold my sixth Rolls with, I might add, a heavy heart. The personalised number plate, which I transferred to each new Rolls, had become so well known that on several occasions the car was vandalised by yobbos. Somebody who was very keen to own the number plate made me an offer I couldn't possibly refuse.

All this happened because a couple of happy drunks stopped by a Rolls Royce showroom in Berkeley Square – and not a nightingale in sight. If I had guessed that the number plate was going to keep me in clover in my old age, I'd have sent that salesman *two* cases of whisky!

Along the way I bought some vintage cars that gave me a great deal of pleasure. One was a 1935 Rolls that had been owned by a blind person in Torquay. It was strange how I became the owner. There is, or was, an auction room in Torquay, which I was passing one morning in 1961. Outside were some stone tubs that I decided would look just beautiful at the house I had bought in Thatcher Avenue, so I went in and sat at the back of the room, looking through the catalogue, waiting for the stone tubs to come up. There were quite a few items to go before the bidding began.

I had seen parked outside a 1935 Landaulette Rolls Royce, and that was one of the items being auctioned. The bidding started at £500, then slowly climbed to £700. There were no more bids, and the auctioneer begged, 'Come on ladies and gentlemen . This car is a Rolls Royce. Who will make it £750?' Nobody stirred. I raised my hand. 'Any more offers?' Not a dicky bird from the small gathering. 'Sold to the gentleman at the back for £750.' That was me. Bang went the gavel and I became the reluctant owner of the RR. After I had paid I put the four stone tubs in the back and drove my purchases up to the new house we had named 'Coppertop' (cos the roof was made of solid copper, see?).

Blossom looked at me in disbelief. 'What are you going to do with *two* Rolls Royces?' she asked. I didn't have an answer because I didn't know.

But let me tell you about my 'folly' For the next fifteen years, the family enjoyed excursions into the country in that car, complete with hampers and champagne, because the Landaulette held seven very comfortably. We went kite-flying, fishing on the River Test, spent weekends at Henley and so much more. As it was a thirties' model I had a tape player fitted and played cassettes by Ambrose, Harry Roy, Jack Hylton and singers from that era. The car had been painted the yellow of the automobile in that wonderful movie with Ingrid Bergman, *The Yellow Rolls Royce*. It caught every eye.

When the time came to part with it, a buyer in Bournemouth paid me £25,000 for 'Old Yellow'. Not bad for a car I had paid less than £1,000 for. Of course not all vintage cars make that kind of profit . . .

A few years ago, my son Anthony told me of a vintage Daimler that had belonged to King George VI – Prince Philip had inherited the car when the king died, but had found that his knees touched the dashboard. The present owner in Cornwall was keen to sell it and wanted £25,000. I bought it and placed it in the hands of Hoopers, the car-body builders.

Why I remember Bill Stickers.

My thanks to magician Chris Woodward for conjuring up these past posters from older shows – there were more, but modesty forbids.

Out of Town
Words and Music by
LESLIE BRICUSSE & ROBIN BEAUMONT

COLIN LESSLIE
presents
MAX BYGRAVES
DENNIS PRICE · MICHAEL MEDWIN
in
"CHARLEY MOON"
COLOUR BY
EASTMAN COLOUR
with
SHIRLEY EATON · PATRICIA DRISCOLL · REGINALD BECKWITH
CYRIL RAYMOND · CHARLES VICTOR & FLORENCE DESMOND

A COLIN LESSLIE PRODUCTION

EDWARD KASSNER MUSIC CO. LTD · LOND.

LONDON PALLADIUM
6·15 TWICE NIGHTLY 8·45 OPENS OCT. 21ST MAT. WEDS. AT 2·40
OUR 1952 BIG AUTUMN SHOW
WONDERFUL TIME
BILLY COTTON AND HIS BAND
JOY NICHOLS STAR OF "TAKE IT FROM HERE"
MAX BYGRAVES I'VE ARRIVED AND TO PROVE IT I'M HERE
JOHN TILLER GIRLS
VADJA DEL ORO
THREE GHEZZI BROS
ELIANE & RODOLPH
GEORGE AND BERT BERNARD OUR AMERICAN GUEST ARTISTES
JO, JAC & JONI

LONDON PALLADIUM
VAL PARNELL & BERNARD DELFONT present
OPENS MAY 21
6·15 Twice Nightly 8·45
MAX BYGRAVES
in A NEW HAPPY-GO-LUCKY REVUE
SWINGING DOWN THE LANE
PRODUCED BY ROBERT NESBITT
PETERS SISTERS
BOB WILLIAMS
ROB MURRAY
ELIZABETH LARNER
SCHALLER BROS
HARRY JACOBSON
HOPE & KEEN
GEORGE CARDEN'S BOYS & GIRLS
ALETA MORRISON

THE 1957 LONDON PALLADIUM SHOW
6·15 TWICE NIGHTLY 8·45
VAL PARNELL & BERNARD DELFONT
MAX BYGRAVES
WHO SAYS "WE'RE HAVING A BALL"
WITH
JOAN REGAN
THE GOOFERS FIRST APPEARANCE IN ENGLAND · NEW GREAT AMERICAN COMEDY ACT

LAST WEEKS
MUST TERMINATE SAT. 14TH DEC.
OPENING 23RD DECEMBER
VAL PARNELL'S 9th MAGNIFICENT PANTOMIME
'ROBINSON CRUSOE'
BIG HEARTED ARTHUR ASKEY
THE TERRIFIC CAST INCLUDES
DAVID WHITFIELD
TOMMY COOPER

FAMOUS LONDON PALLADIUM
2·30 TWICE DAILY 7·0
VAL PARNELL'S 7th MAGNIFICENT
PANTOMIME
MOTHER GOOSE
BOOK BY PHIL PARK
MAX BYGRAVES
MARGARET BURTON
BALLETS ARRANGED BY PAULINE GRANT
SHIRLEY EATON
AIDA FOSTER BABES
PETER SELLERS
GEORGE MITCHELL SINGERS
THE NITWITS
HARRY CRANLEY
AILEEN COCHRANE
LES MATHURINS
ALAN TOWNSEND
"MR. PASTRY"
RICHARD HEARNE
DECOR BY CHARLES READING
STAGED BY CHARLES HENRY

Left 'Have drum, will travel' – Anthony and I off to Hong Kong.

Below With daughter Christine in Hawaii.

Above This is a picture of a divine god – and the other one's a statue!

Below Sightseeing in Hong Kong with my driver – Rick Shaw.

Right Aboard the QE2 – what a pleasure craft.

This is me in 'Koala' lumpar.

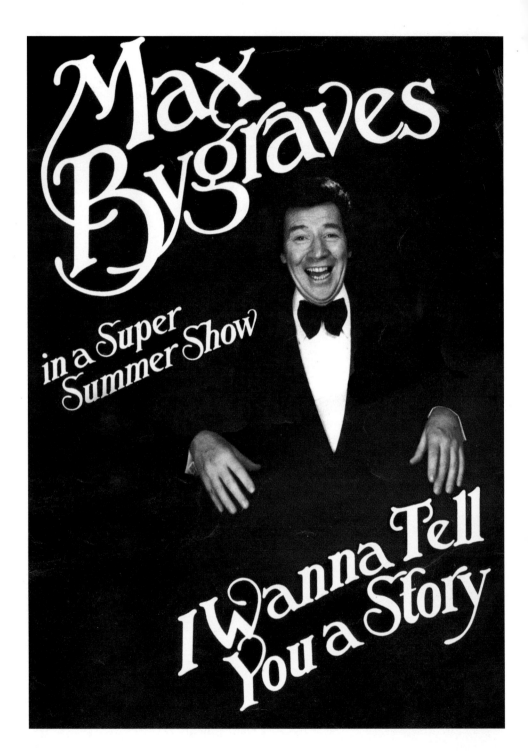

Everybody does an impression of me – I once went in for a competition for who does it best – and came fifth.

Above Put it there – and yes, you can have my tickets for the Cup Final.

Below Me, Bloss and Mr and Mrs Michael Caine, and I'm saying, 'Not a lot of people know that!'…

A bevvy of Beverleys – one of the most professional singing groups I have worked with.

They worked on it for five months, and brought it up to showroom condition at a cost of £50,000. After the restoration I found that my knees touched the dashboard too, and had to spend another £3,000 to fix the problem. The end of this sad story is that Sotheby's sold the Daimler for £45,000, and after commission and many extras I finished up almost £33,000 out of pocket.

So if you are going into the vintage car market, think twice. But remember that if you want to be a *real* star you must have a Rolls Royce – it goes with the territory. You will also need a longer garage, a chauffeur and a relief driver, plus an experienced mechanic on hand. Then if your chauffeur is lucky enough to find an empty parking meter and has change to stop the ticket wardens, you can have a wonderful two hours shopping up at Harrods. You are a star – good luck to you.

There *is* a happy ending here. When I parted with all my luxury cars to settle down with a reliable Rover, I sold the personalised number plate MB 1 for £100,000. A friend, Mark Bryant, decided to try to trace the number for his wife, whose name is Mary Bryant, and discovered that my buyer was now asking £250,000 – a quarter of a million pounds! 'Oh Max, you fool, why didn't you wait?' But you can't wait, not when you are notching up eighty years. I'll stay with my bike now.

*

Another memory worth sharing concerns a trip on the *QE2* from Southampton to New York, a six-day journey following the route (almost) of the *Titanic*. It was memorable for me because a large number of the passengers were vintage car owners. They were travelling to the US to sell by auction some of the automobiles that made up a large part of the ship's cargo.

After I had done my act in cabaret to a very receptive audience I was approached by the Cruise Director. He had heard I was the owner of a vintage car, the Daimler that had once belonged to King George VI. He asked if I would say a few words the next day to the passengers about the old car, which had first been registered in 1936. I told the Cruise Director it would be a pleasure.

Thinking I would share the stage with several other vintage car owners, I made my way next day to the crowded ballroom. It was a shock to discover there were no other speakers – only me. I was down to speak for half an hour. To fill thirty minutes with chat completely unrehearsed seemed like a marathon. I told the Cruise Director I could manage six or seven minutes perhaps, but to entertain the crowded ballroom for half an hour would be impossible.

The Cruise Director felt sure I would manage. I asked him to 'feed' me with questions such as, 'How did you purchase your first Rolls Royce?' and then go on to 'When did you get the second?' Making these questions mile-stones, I reckoned I had a few 'stories' I could remember about owning RRs, all with the number plate MB 1.

I found I had lots of stories of 'Life with a Rolls'. One was when I was taking part in a charity golf match at Moor Park. I'd finished the match to find a young lad sitting by my car with an autograph book at the ready. 'Do you want my autograph, son?' I asked. 'No,' he said. 'I'm waiting for *him*,' pointing at my number plate MB 1. 'Who's him?' I asked. 'Michael Barrymore,' said the lad. Exit me, with my tail between my legs.

Many more stories came to mind. Eventually, the Cruise Director, looking at his watch, told the audience we'd have to leave it there as lunch was being served. There were some 'Oh no's' and then very generous applause. I asked how long I had been on and was *amazed* to learn the session had lasted one hour and twenty minutes! And we were only up to my fourth RR. When I told Eric Sykes this story he said, 'Did you mention that MB 1 stood for Max the Bullsh. . .er First Class?'

SIRS, LORDS AND GENTLEMEN

When I think of some of the stars who have made me blink in wonderment, I realise that just meeting them briefly was enough to fix the memory for ever. Sometimes I come across their names in an article, or hear a mention on TV, that catches my attention, and I am off down memory lane . . .

*

Driving down the M3 earlier in the week I was listening to Jimmy Young, who is around about my age. I always marvel at his professionalism, his keenness for his job, his eagerness to please with a programme always full of entertainment, a rare thing on radio nowadays.

I have known Sir Jimmy for most of my working life, have done interviews with him on his programme and had drinks at the bar with him. I think that all he wants to do in life is to make his programme the best he can, and doesn't the BBC know it. To me Jim is irreplaceable. He is loved by listeners because he is the best – nobody does it better. It may seem like off-the-cuff broadcasting, but it is hard work by back room staff that keeps the old lad up-to-date with current affairs and in on-air interviews with experts who try to answer today's troubling questions.

Let's not forget that Sir James started life as a better-than-average crooner. Like myself, he played the halls, both the big time and the dumps. He is a survivor – not a doddling old-timer, fishing for words and conversation. Jimmy is an articulate, friendly soul enjoying the fruits of a life devoted to the public. I'm sure when the day comes, as it will with all of us, he will look back contented. Keep going, Jim. You are a true gentleman.

*

Norman Hartnell, the Queen's dressmaker, is a gentleman if ever there was one. We met in the foyer of the Palladium after a Royal Command show I had appeared in. For my spot I had worn a charcoal grey suit, white shirt and yellow tie. Yellow ties are worn quite a lot now, but rarely then.

Mr Hartnell liked my colour scheme and remarked what a good ensemble it made. I was flattered as he was the man who made 'frocks' for Her Majesty. Several days later, I was in Bond Street and walking towards me was Mr Hartnell. We stopped to say hello, he mentioned the yellow tie I'd worn at the Palladium earlier in the week.

He was surprised when I told him that on arriving home that night I found the tie was missing. I ventured that some 'so and so' had 'half inched' (pinched) it. He loved to use rhyming slang too – he told me not to worry, he'd make me another 'Peckham Rye'. We parted and several days later I received an invitation from him for lunch at his salon just off Bond Street, to honour his friend, the novelist and celebrity Dame Barbara Cartland.

At a table for ten, we sat down to an all-pink luncheon: pink tablecloth and napkins, pink roses in the middle of the table. Dame Barbara was in a pink creation by Sir Norman, the waiters wore pink jackets and, would you believe, the first course was pink soup, made with strawberries. It was delicious.

I think the only thing that wasn't pink was Dame Barbara's black eyelashes. They fluttered so often we didn't need the air-conditioning on. She didn't stop talking but at least it was chatter that was interesting. No wonder she had been able to write some 140 books – best-sellers too.

As we were leaving, Sir Norman asked me to linger a while. I waited until the others had all left and then Sir Norman returned with a gift for me. I opened the pink wrapping to find not one but two yellow ties, both in a different shade of yellow. I wear them often, particularly on TV – there is no other colour more favourable for the cameras. And of course they have the tag that reads 'Norman Hartnell'.

I had a call from Sir Norman after a TV show I did. He remarked, 'I noticed you were wearing one of the ties – didn't you like the other one?' Sly humour, eh?

*

Today, as I write, the Sunday papers are filled with Jeffrey Archer stories. It must be an editor's dream at this time of year, with the political stage empty and not much going on except for some stone-throwing at a summit in Genoa. Pride of place is given to Jeffrey Archer's past, regurgitated over and over.

Almost everybody who has ever spoken to Lord Archer, even if only a few words, write of his colourful past. It made me search some old letter files to remember what his lordship had written to me about.

I first met Lord Archer at the opening night of *Chicago* at the Adelphi Theatre. He was seated directly in front of me in the next row. During the interval he didn't go to the bar, but turned to scan the audience still seated. I'd met him before and he turned to me and said, 'Hello Max, my boy. How are you?' We chatted for a few minutes and then he said, 'Come on, let's have a drink'. We left our ladies, my wife Blossom and Lady Archer, and entered the crowded bar. With little chance of getting served, he saw somebody he knew and made his way over to them. I never saw him again until we took our seats for the second half of the show. We had another little chat, and that was the last meeting I ever had with him. I didn't get the drink he asked me to have, but the moment is indelible in my memory.

In three or four minutes I felt I had known him for ages. I liked him tremendously and liked Lady Archer even more. My wife, a good reader of character, liked her ladyship too, enough to say later what a really nice person she was.

What did we chat about? I mentioned that the flat he was living in, the one that looks east up the Thames, was the same one I had gone to buy thirty-odd years before. 'How much were they asking then?' was his first question. I told him that in those days the price for the lease was £27,000. He looked over his glasses to tell me that today's price was half a million pounds for the same apartment. He then enquired what stopped me from purchasing the property. I didn't have the nerve to tell him why. This was the reason . . .

The occupant was a charming and beautiful singer of the time, married to the musical and talented John Barry. After she had shown us around we were almost sold, but first said we'd like to see the garage space. We descended in the lift to the ground floor parking area. It was a cold day with an icy wind blowing. As we turned the corner to the car park, I almost stumbled over a middle-aged couple lying on a sheepskin coat, doing what comes naturally. The woman saw me and whispered, 'Joe – get off!'

Joe was obviously at the point of no return, and just went on with the bonking, his bare bottom exposed to the elements. My wife choked back an 'Oh my God!' and went into reverse, murmuring, 'How could they? And on a Sunday too!' Later on, she mentioned that had we been police, they could have gone to prison. I remember my pianist's thoughts on the subject: 'a standing penis has no conscience.'

It was that experience that put us off buying the flat.

Lord Archer will be able to enjoy it again soon. A report a few days ago said he had managed to write two more books while inside. If *Stars In My Eyes* does half as well as his books usually do, I'll buy him that drink he nearly bought me at the theatre.

MUSIC, MAESTRO, PLEASE

Victor Sylvester has such a distinctive sound. You have no need to ask who it is when you hear the tinkling piano, the solo Oscar Grasso on violin and the strict tempo that people loved to dance to 'in the old-fashioned way'.

Victor never normally used vocalists, but the boss of Pye records, for whom I was recording at the time, suggested that it might be an idea for Victor to feature a 'vocal refrain', as they put it, on the old records of Jack Hylton, Ambrose and dance orchestras of yesteryear. I would supply the songs – my sale of LPs was huge – with Victor and his unmistakable sound, it seemed a good sales pitch, and it was.

I had met Victor at a couple of awards shows and, like everybody, loved his style of music. I remember hearing it first during the war on *Music While You Work*, the BBC programme that was supposed to keep factory workers happy. It *did* work because they seemed to turn out better munitions when Victor's music was played. It was basic music – no complicated orchestrations, simple but so effective, especially for those amateur dancers who fancied themselves as the Astaire–Rogers of the ballroom.

Victor and I met at a rehearsal room near Marble Arch. The arranger of the music made the introductions and we eyed each other, me in my sports jacket and flannels, Victor in his tailored street clothes (Savile Row). His first words were: 'There's nobody I would rather make music with.' That remark made us friends for ever.

The first thing that struck me about VS was his 'know how', his suggestions for titles that would be standard tunes but not too old for the modern record buyer, *or* too new. Also, he insisted that the songs should have strong melody lines.

We set to work routining numbers like 'Tie a Yellow Ribbon' and 'Dance in the Old-fashioned Way', both current at that time. And we added Irving Berlin's 'What'll I Do' and a couple more waltzes.

I always looked forward to the 'breaks' in the coffee bar when we would talk about sport. I was most surprised to find him a keen football fan. He would talk of some obscure players he had seen playing for Grimsby Town or a third division player to look out for, adding 'that boy's going places'. At one break he made a good case for the Americans getting into soccer and said that if they do they will commandeer the game. I asked him why he thought that and he replied, 'Because they've got the money.'

This was in the seventies when football wasn't the game it is today. His one dread seemed to be that the game as we knew it would change for the worse when the men in suits started controlling the purse strings. What a prophecy. Can't you see it happening here in the UK now?

*

If you were ever lucky enough to catch a 'live' performance of the Joe Loss Band you couldn't fail to have enjoyed it. Joe had a commanding way with a reticent audience. He'd say, 'Ladies and gentlemen, most of the men in my band have devoted their lives to making perfect music for you to enjoy. We have just travelled two hundred miles [even if they hadn't] by road to be here. You have paid good money to enjoy our music, so don't be reluctant to grab a partner and have a good time! Get on the dance floor, throw away your cares and tear it up – cut a rug – boogie – anything – but do enjoy it!'

That pep talk always worked. As he finished talking Joe would raise his baton and go into a modern rendering of the day's latest hit. The brass would blare and the drums beat out the rhythm. By the end of the first chorus the shy audience would be transformed into extroverts. That's why Joe outperformed every other band for almost sixty years.

We worked together for the first time in 1949 at the Sunderland Empire, and became friends. One of my earliest attempts at song-writing was a comedy number entitled 'The Brave Slave of Turkey'. Joe had his arranger take it down note for note from me, and a few nights later his vocalist Howard Jones featured it on the Saturday night show. I had never heard a song of mine played on anything but a piano. That night the flutes and clarinets plus the drums and percussion made my simple tune come to life. The following week Joe featured it in one of his BBC broadcasts. What a thrill.

The song wasn't a hit, but I was so grateful to Joe for even considering my effort, especially one that sounded horribly like snake-charmer music with lyrics. I can only remember the opening lines:

> In Turkey land not long ago
> Lived Sultan Mystaphilipo
> *The Sultan had about three thousand wives . . .*

The pay-off was 'He also had three thousand mothers-in-law', which of course meant that the Sultan wasn't all that lucky.

*

The easiest money I ever made was with the gimmick of 'Singalong a Max'. Before that, for almost thirty years, I made a lot of records. Some entered the Top Ten – you may remember 'You Need Hands' and 'Tulips from Amsterdam', and let's not forget 'You're a pink toothbrush, I'm a blue toothbrush'. Those that weren't big hits still sold well to my fans and my records were played on radio by prominent disc jockeys such as Pete Murray, David Jacobs and Jimmy Young. Unfortunately things changed and the airwaves seemed to be taken over with 'youth' music – rock and roll – with the same sounds, banal lyrics and a heavy beat.

Like me, the older buyers of music weren't much interested in the new sounds. So nearing the age of forty I decided I needed to change my recording style. It was a stroke of luck that put me back in the best sellers for the next ten years. With the simple title of 'Singalong a Max', which was thought up by bandleader and recording manager Cyril Stapleton, we found a public that was being ignored by the recording industry. These recordings outsold Sinatra, Presley and Crosby – the publication *Music Week*, which published the Top Ten every week, were flabbergasted by the sales. At one period there were three of our albums in the Top Twenty, four in the Top Thirty. I had never made so much money so easily.

It was a simple format: a rhythm section and familiar songs sung by a group of professional singers led by Tony Mansell, with arrangements by Frank Barber. The sound engineer Terry Everett produced these infectious recordings, with words and music by some of the great songwriters, such as Irving Berlin, Cole Porter and Hoagy Carmichael. There was an inexhaustible supply of songs from the music companies in Tin Pan Alley. They never stopped thanking me for the royalties that poured in for songs that they thought had enjoyed better days.

The stroke of luck I mentioned was the day I called at my

mother's house in Welling, Kent. The two things she liked most were to sing to herself while cooking or dusting and the success I was having as a regular performer at London's Palladium. She would often call me from a pub called The Rose in Welling to ask if I could fix a couple of seats for herself and a friend at the Palladium. It was always my pleasure to do this for such a wonderful lady, and even though she had already seen the show six or seven times she enthused as if it were the first time. She brought her friends to show me off – 'her son backstage in his dressing room'.

Back to the day I called at the semi-detached in Welling ... My mother opened the door and the first thing I noticed was how quiet it was. She usually had the 'wireless' turned up too loud, so much so that I had to turn the volume down before we could speak. But this day all was quiet. 'What's the matter, Ma? Is the wireless on the blink?' I asked. She shrugged, saying, 'The music seems to be all bomp-bomp-bomp. There's nothing being played that I know.'

Mum didn't realise that the programmes she enjoyed, such as *Music While You Work* and *Housewives' Choice*, were being phased out and The Beatles were coming in with a vengeance. For the first time in many years, professional musicians were struggling – orchestras and dance bands were being replaced by trios or quartets. With electronic mastering these much smaller 'groups' could be deafening. 'Echo' or 'verb' could be added to the sound and any vocalist singing out of tune could be a hit. Suddenly we were in the electronic age. Artistes either had to fall in or be left by the wayside.

Knowing I was going into the studio for a recording session later that week, I told Mum not to worry. I'd put down a track or two with some of her favourite songs and let her have the tape to play on her cassette player.

I forget which track we were recording in the studio that week, but we finished earlier than expected. I had a word with the sound engineer Terry Everett and told him I was going to record a few songs for my mother, with pianist Bob Dixon tinkling away. Bob, who had been with me for many years, knew most of my keys to sing in. In no time I was vocalising some of those oldies that my mother's age group were familiar with – 'When the Red Red Robin comes bob bob bobbing along' sequed into 'Won't you come home, Bill Bailey', which sequed into 'Oh, You Beautiful Doll'.

A couple of the musicians joined in. Cyril Stapleton came out of the recording booth smiling and said, 'Hey, that's not a bad sound. It's a long time since there was a good old sing-song on record. We ought to make it.' A week or two later we did exactly that, with some top session singers. They were happy to be singing good lyrics again instead of just the oohs and aahs on the other popular records being turned out.

The young disc jockeys weren't interested in the first *Singalong a Max* album. The older generation loved the sound but agreed it was old-fashioned. But a little later, on my television programme *Max*, my orchestra leader Geoff Love presented me with a gold disc from Astor Records for sales of *Singalong a Max* in Australia. We were still live on air when Geoff asked me, in front of millions of viewers, if I had ever received a gold disc for my recordings. 'Never', I said. The gold record honestly was a surprise.

We were taping the show for a later date. I gave the nod to Bob Dixon, who went into the opening bars of 'Me and My Shadow'. The singers with the choir joined in, and so did the audience. The technicians kept the cameras turning and we ended up with four minutes of unrehearsed material that when pieced together for the recorded TV show fitted as if planned.

On the transmission date, the switchboards at Thames TV came alive with viewers asking where they could purchase the album. The rest is history.

*

For the obituary I wrote in the *Guardian* on Geoff Love (10 July 1991), the heading was 'Love – a many splendoured man'. I tried to put into words the deep affection and respect I had, and still feel, for the lovely Geoff.

We first met in the early fifties. In those days Geoff was an arranger and I was recording for the HMV label. I was to record a song titled 'Meet Me On the Corner'. The record was a hit, a Top Ten entry, equally because of Geoff's fine arrangement. It was so successful we named a show after it, which had a long run at the London Hippodrome.

After that Geoff and I saw each other occasionally over the years. Then in 1972 Thames TV asked me to appear in a series to be called simply *Max*. I was told I could have my choice of orchestra leaders, and without hesitation I plumped for Geoff Love. So started a partnership on TV that lasted over fifteen years.

This was in the days before accountants became the top men in television, when we got paid for performing; nowadays the bottom line rules. The only appearance a performer is asked to make now is as a guest on a chat show. The host will pick up £5,000,000 per annum, while the artiste can look forward to 'expenses'. In Australia it's even worse – not only are you expected to arrive under your own steam, but also to spend hours rehearsing and in make-up, to provide your own material, and generally to make the host look good. All this just for a plug! I was having dinner once with Ronnie Corbett and Danny La Rue and we were asking each other how Australian Equity permits this sort of racket. None of us had an answer.

Back to Geoff, who had trouble rolling his r's. For our back-chat, the writers (unknown to Geoff) would write a line full of r's like 'The Rolls Royce is round on the ramp'. When Geoff delivered the line it came out, 'The Wolls Woyce is wound on the wamp!' Sometimes, to get an extra laugh, I'd say, 'Geoff, would you mind wepeating that.'

Geoff also recorded as Manuel of the Mountains. His records sold in large numbers down Argentina way. He also provided backings for Shirley Bassey, Russ Conway and many more top recording stars of the day. In between he gave his time to Stars Organisation for Spastics (SOS).

His happiest days were spent in Spain. When work permitted he would get into his Jaguar with his lovely wife Joyce and snatch a few days at Sitges, south of Barcelona. On return he'd show off his suntan. As he was the grandson of a Cherokee Indian, the suntan was hard to see, but he assured us it was there. Even Joyce, a born and bred English lady, would shake her head in disbelief.

On one of his last trips going over to Spain he was mugged. It happened just outside Lyons in France. He was flagged down by a 'conman' in another car. When Geoff stopped, the conman pointed to the back wheel, so Geoff got out to see what was wrong. Suddenly an accomplice jumped in the driving seat of Geoff's car, turned the key and was away with the Jaguar plus all Geoff's belongings, passport, money etc.

Geoff told me all this over the phone when he arrived back in England. 'I don't suppose you will feel like going back to Spain again, will you Geoff?' I asked. 'Oh, yes', he replied, 'I don't feel the same without a tan.'

SONGS AND WRITERS

A question often asked is whether the entertainment industry has changed since I first trod the boards. Well, one of the obvious factors for me is that humour has gone from the song market. Our 'Tin Pan Alley' – Denmark Street, just off Charing Cross Road – was alive with songwriters who always 'had the very song' in their back pockets, whatever kind of song you wanted.

Tell one of these songwriters you needed a song about love or happiness or a woman's tears and, if they didn't have such a song, they'd say meet me here tomorrow. The following day they would be there with the manuscript in hand. They'd have organised a piano in some publisher's office (there were some twenty or more music publishers in the street). You'd be steered into the office and the writer would sit at the piano to play a piece that he had probably worked on through the night.

This happened to me several times and some good songs came my way. You may find it hard to believe that a song I recorded, which still enjoys good sales, was actually composed by *four* (you haven't read that wrong) professional songwriters. One of them was Dick James, who later published most of The Beatles' songs. Can you imagine it took four grown men to write:

> You're a pink toothbrush
> I'm a blue toothbrush
> Have we met somewhere before?
> You're a pink toothbrush
> And I think, toothbrush
> That we met by the bathroom door
>
> Glad to meet toothbrush
> Such a sweet toothbrush
> How you thrill me through and through
> Don't be hard toothbrush
> On a soft toothbrush
> Cos I can't help loving you
>
> Every time I hear you whistle [whistle]
> It makes my nylon bristle
> You're a pink toothbrush
> I'm a blue toothbrush
> Won't you marry me in haste?
> I'll be true toothbrush
> Just to you toothbrush
> When we both use the same toothpaste

Sometimes in my stage act I'll announce a request for this song. If I hear a ripple go through the audience I'll add, 'Don't knock it, folks. That song has sold over three million. Not records – toothbrushes.'

In my day there was an insatiable demand for these sorts of songs and I was able to plug them in the song spot of the radio show *Educating Archie*. I had the field mostly to myself because the established singers and crooners stayed away from this type of material. David Whitfield stuck to ballads like 'Cara Mia', and Dickie Valentine was concentrating on Ted Heath Band numbers. Sometimes vocal quartets like The Stargazers would do a chorus of 'Where will the Baby's Dimple be', but mostly the novelty songs were left to me.

It makes me smile when I think of what the recording company handed me to record. How about this one: 'Put away the chip chopper, Charlie, we're frying the guv'nor tonight . . .'

> . . . he was in the kitchen
> Chopping up chips
> When he stuck his foot out
> And suddenly slips
> Right into the boiling hot dripping
> He tumbled in heels over head
> So put away the chip chopper Charlie
> We're frying the guv'nor instead . . .

And they got worse! What about 'When you come to the end of a lollipop', and 'Gilly Gilly Ossenfeffer Katchenellen Bogan by the Sea'. There were many titles I am almost too ashamed to mention – 'I haven't had a bang since bonfire night' . . . so I won't mention it.

There is a story about Tin Pan Alley that is in the Michael-Caine's-'Not-a-lot-of-people-know-that' mould. And it's true. It goes like this . . .

You might remember back in the sixties there was a television pop show called *The Old Grey Whistle Test*. It is interesting how the title was originated. In the early days of songwriting there was a great deal of competition and writers would often spend all night in their publisher's office, banging on the piano, trying to find the next big hit song of the day. One of their acid tests was to ask the morning cleaner, who invariably wore grey overalls, to listen to their latest masterpiece and then whistle it back. If the cleaner could do this successfully the writer knew he had written something catchy and memorable, something that probably had the chance of becoming a hit. And this was called 'The old grey whistle test'. Just thought you'd like to know that.

There was a songwriter I was very fond of. He was short, modest and very clever with his lyrics. His name was Jack Meadows. I had created a catchphrase on radio – 'Big 'ead' – and when it caught on with the nation, Jack was there with a song titled 'Big 'ead'. We sold a lot of records until a letter to a newspaper gave a different interpretation to the composition.

I was blamed for taking a rise from people afflicted with a deformity. Nothing was further from my mind – my version was aimed at conceited and pompous people. The writers and producers hadn't misunderstood the song either. If they *had*, the BBC and the record companies would never have sanctioned it. But I still had to soft pedal, and 'Big 'ead' became extinct. To this day I get mail asking me to include it in my repertoire.

> Why does everybody call me Big 'ead?
> Why do they take the mickey out of me?
> Everywhere I go they call me Big 'ead
> It isn't very nice you must agree
> I don't know how I got the name of Big 'ead
> It's a puzzle that I never could define
> Cos nearly all the folks who call me Big 'ead
> Have got bigger heads than mine

Maybe I missed the point when leading the audience in a sing-along of that song. It was after this I got round to writing and singing my own words and music.

One of my early attempts was while appearing in a show

at the London Palladium. I enjoyed the company of a show-stopping act, still around today and still enjoyable to watch: the Clarke Brothers. Steve and Jimmy are fellow Water Rats and are held in high esteem by that wonderful fellowship.

Between the matinee and evening performance I had penned a rough guide to a song. I was seated at the piano, trying to piece the chorus together, when Steve and Jimmy sidled up. I sang them the lyric, which they immediately began to harmonise with. To cut a long story, I asked the director if we could include the song in the show. It wasn't easy to get permission as the show was already running and had been approved by the Lord Chancellor's Office – in other words 'approved censorship'.

But all the problems were overcome and we three performed the song, Steve and Jimmy on either side of me, all of us wearing gloves. The gloves were treated so that when the lights went to black out and the ultraviolet bulbs came on, the gloves lit up. It was a great effect in the early fifties. The song I'd written was 'You Need Hands' and it became one of the big songs in the show 'Swinging Down the Lane'.

You Need Hands
Words and music Max Bygraves
Publishers Lakeview Music

You need hands
To show the world you're happy
You need hands
To show that you're sincere
When you feel nobody wants to know you
You need hands
To brush away the tear

You need hands
To hold a brand new baby

You need tender hands
To guide them on their way
You need hands
To thank the Lord for living
And for giving us this day

[verses written for stage version]

You need hands
To show the world you're happy
You need hands
When you have to stop the bus
But the hands we love so dear
Are the hands we love to hear
Are the hands that you give to us
The hands that you you give to us

The song was later recorded in US by singer Eydie Gormé and proved a big hit. Its success made Decca Records think about me recording a different type of song, and that's when I followed with an enormous hit that brought me my first gold single. It was 'Tulips from Amsterdam'. It could have been a novelty song, but in fact it was covered by many recording artistes all over the world.

Up until then, the song played most in Holland was 'The Zuider Zee', but once 'Tulips' hit the airwaves it seemed to become their national anthem. It is a catchy tune with a smart sensible lyric and will be around for a good many future years – or my name isn't Max Van der Welde Bygraves.

It is worth a reminder here that I entered show business as a comedy impressionist. Most of my act was a take-off of performers like Hutch, the Ink Spots, Al Jolson and country singer Frankie Laine. Then I composed a song called 'The Cowpuncher's Cantata', a concoction of songs by the great Frankie Laine. All the titles were mixed up, but segued into a comedy conclusion. It entered the very first Top Ten of

UK hit records to be published and stayed there for the next sixteen weeks. Nowadays, songs don't last in the hit parade for sixteen hours, so sixteen weeks in the best sellers was a great accomplishment. It still makes me proud.

From then on, most of my act was geared towards the musical side. Although I didn't have hits as big as 'Hands' or 'Tulips', I was writing more and more music for my act. That paid off in many ways. One was that I didn't have to wonder whether another performer was singing the same song – which did happen and often led to arguments – and another, I was able to feel I was giving fresh ideas to an audience.

*

Leslie Bricusse is a songsmith with Oscars and various other awards galore. His compositions include 'Talk to the Animals', 'What Kind of Fool am I', 'Gonna Build a Mountain' (with Anthony Newley) and so many more. They have made Leslie a very rich man. But his first big hit was 'Out of Town', which he wrote with Robin Beaumont for a movie I made back in the 1950s called *Charley Moon*. Lyrics like 'troubles there're so much rarer, out of town . . .' showed from an early start that this young fellow, fresh from Cambridge, was heading for the 'big time'.

We lived near each other then. In those days Leslie could only afford a two-seater Heinkel, in which he drove his beautiful wife-to-be, Yvonne Romaine, but there was no way Leslie was going to remain poor.

He talked me into becoming a partner in a restaurant to be called 'Maxim's', at Stanmore on the northern outskirts of London. He arranged for two of his buddies to join us, one to become maître 'd' and the other, who'd managed a small wine store in Stanmore, as a partner. We put a lot of time and effort into Maxim's, hoping it would beat all other restaurants in the area. But even though we had the set designer from the early James Bond movies to do the décor, fine wines from the wine merchant Leslie Clarke, and a smiling and welcoming manager in Brian Barnett, it never really took off. We didn't make anything from the hard work we put into it. John Bloom, the washing-machine tycoon, was one of our best customers. I often think we might have made a go of it, if Harold Wilson hadn't put the block on tax-free lunches!

In the meantime, Leslie had found a partner for his songwriting skills with Anthony Newley. They wrote *Stop the World I Want to Get Off* and *Pickwick* plus some lucrative deals Leslie secured with the James Bond pictures, notably *Goldfinger*. In the early days Leslie found his way to Hollywood and gave lavish parties for anybody that mattered, especially anybody who could perform his songs, including Sammy Davis Jnr and Liza Minnelli. Leslie moved to the South of France. He was a quiet but successful operator. With Yvonne his stunning wife he threw the best parties you could ever be lucky enough to attend.

Just before Anthony Newley died, I was talking to the very friendly Sammy Davis Jnr. We both mentioned that we hadn't seen Leslie for quite some time. Sammy then said, 'I guess he's travelling the world, looking for some tax-free island.'

Incidentally, one day I received a gold-embossed invitation through the post. It was from my former partners Brian Barnett and Leslie Clarke, who had opened a chain of liquor stores known as 'Augustus Barnett'. The party was in honour of their hundreth store to be opened. They sold out later, and now own racehorses. So don't try to open a posh restaurant in the Stanmore area. Here endeth the lesson.

*

Lionel Bart confessed to me once that he had found real fame when his name was included in the Cockney Rhyming Slang dictionary: a 'Lionel Bart' was the name for a noisy stomach disorder. He was elated to have heard a comedian once tell about a society madam at a posh do tearing off a 'Lionel Bart'.

Being a cockney from London's East End, Lionel

appreciated this as the ultimate accolade. Never mind that he was famous for writing the musical *Oliver*, with a little help from Dickens, and songs for top performers such as Tommy Steele and Shirley Bassey plus quite a few others. Never mind the many trophies for his songwriting skills. Lionel just adored being included in language used by the East End gangs such as the Kray Twins and the Richardson mob.

Over the years we got to know each other very well, and my company Lakeview Music bought the score of *Oliver*. This came about when Lionel brought an old-fashioned Grundig recording machine into my office. He put on a spool of tape and I sat there for the next hour listening to the whole score, amounting to some sixteen songs.

The words didn't make a lot of sense without the dialogue, but Lionel furnished this between the numbers. One song, however, really grabbed my attention; it was 'Consider Yourself'. I could visualise a pack of urchins in a Victorian workhouse performing this to an audience. The rest of the songs I admit that I found rather pedestrian.

'What are you selling for?' I asked Lionel. 'I've had an offer from Jimmy Philips of £300 [he hadn't], but if you can better it . . .' To cut a long story short, I bought the entire score for £350, which turned out to be a very lucrative deal.

Of course, not every show project is a runaway success. *Oliver* was first shown at the Wimbledon Theatre and was a disaster. Not only were there plenty of empty seats on opening night, it got worse during the short run.

It was a little bit of luck that set *Oliver* on the road to riches. An impresario named Donald Albery owned a theatre, now called the Donald Albery Theatre. He had had a flop there, so at the same time that *Oliver* had come off in Wimbledon, Donald Albery's theatre was 'dark'. Rather than keep the theatre empty, he decided to put on this Dickens musical that was already rehearsed; the music scores were written and ready, the cast were word perfect and permission had been granted for the young urchins to appear on stage.

The production was announced as 'a successful and mind-blowing performance of the Charles Dickens story'. The toast of the theatre world was soon Lionel Bart, and the show *Oliver* brought fame and fortune to all.

My company took a large investment in Lionel's next venture entitled *Twang*, a musical based on the Robin Hood story. It wasn't another *Oliver*, and it came off in a couple of weeks. We lost our entire investment.

Lionel, in the meantime, was living it up. When *Oliver* opened in New York, he not only rented a suite at the top hotel, he also rented an adjoining suite for friends who came to see the show, or were passing through. Money was spent as if there was no end. The last thing he cared about was the tax men wanting their pound of flesh.

Shortly after writing *From Russia with Love* for a James Bond film, Lionel showed me a demand from HM Tax Office. 'We all have to pay if we earn it,' I told him. He then admitted he didn't have the money. Stories like this abound in show business – up one day, down the next. For ages he called our office for advances on his royalty payments, so much so that our accountants asked us to put a block on them. Lionel carried on as if there was no tomorrow. He sold his copyrights. In fact, he sold anything that could keep him away from the bankruptcy court.

Although he was one of my favourite men, and I admired him for his fertile brain and gentle nature, he deteriorated alarmingly towards the end of his life. When he died I was overseas and could not make it to the Jewish cemetery in Golders Green, but I heard that everybody spoke kindly and lovingly about his gift as one of the 'great' songwriters of the world. Consider yourself one of 'em, Lionel.

WANDERING STAR

I have rarely had to pay for holidays because my work has taken me to so many exotic places – San Francisco, the Bahamas, New York, Cape Town, Sydney, New Zealand, several trips on the *QE2* and other luxury liners. In most cases the fares and hotels are paid for by the promoters.

In turn, I perform at venues for them and make them a profit. I cannot remember a date where we didn't make money for the promoters. It is a good arrangement and almost everybody comes out smiling.

Most people who go travelling fill their snapshot albums with photographs of places that bring back memories. But not me. I like to remember the people I meet and to jot down events on the backs of the photos. It seems to be a better subject for talk when those photo albums come out for visitors.

In nearly all my travels I have been able to take my wife and children. Of course, this didn't happen so much in the early days when the kids were at school, but in the later years Blossom has always been with me. I need her expertise at 'getting me ready' – she is really all I have to consult because being a solo act I can do things that I would not do alone. And if she weren't there, I wouldn't think of going to a museum to see a reconstruction of a dinosaur, like we did in Sydney, Australia, or climb to the top of Table Mountain in Cape Town or visit Cecil Rhodes' tomb in Rhodesia (now Zimbabwe). So many things fill my memory book when I look back . . . Let's get the album out and take another look.

How did I get this picture in Sydney Harbour with the lovely Vera Lynn? It was during the visit by Princess Diana and Prince Charles. A wealthy record producer invited us onto his yacht to watch what turned out to be the greatest fireworks display I have ever witnessed. The memory of the entire Harbour Bridge (known as the 'coathanger') being lit up for a finale is something that will remain with me for ever – and the startled look on Princess Di's lovely face.

This one is with Frank Ifield ('I remember you-ooh'). Poor old Frank had a nodule on his throat and doctor's orders were no singing for six months. No singing was like taking the life blood away from him. I'm glad to say he's okay now.

I can see Lionel Abrahams with wife Nicky downing a glass of champagne – agents only drink champers.

The first time I took my family on a holiday using air travel was when we went to Jersey, in the early fifties. The flight took only forty minutes, but the wonderment of it has stayed with my three children to this day. Apart from the trip, an event occurred that still makes us laugh. It concerned Anthony, my son, who was about seven or eight at the time.

When most families gather together, at weddings, funerals, Christmas and similar occasions, there is usually a favourite family story that is trotted out, time and time again. Our family is no exception, and one of the yarns we enjoy most is the tale of Anthony and the wallet.

At the time I liked to crack gags about him 'training to be a miser' – one of my favourite stories was when a tramp knocked at our street door and Anthony answered. The tramp said, 'Any old clothes?' and Anthony replied, 'Yes, please!' . . . We arrived in Jersey on the Saturday. I gave the three children £5 each and told them that was their holiday spending money. The two girls spent half of it over the weekend. Anthony, on the other hand, spent only six-pence, to buy a plastic wallet. In this he put all his remaining money – four pound notes, the ten shilling note and the silver – and he kept it on him at all times. (Today, he is one of the most generous people you could wish to meet, but in those days, he was tighter than a duck's arse – and that's watertight.)

The first night, as we were going to bed, I heard a shrill cry come from the children's bedroom. I rushed in to find Anthony sobbing and our babysitter Phyllis laughing uncontrollably. It took a while to get the story out of her.

This is what happened. Anthony had decided that if burglars came in the night they wouldn't find his wallet if he hid it under the mattress of his bed. After about five minutes he reckoned that was the first place they'd look, so he got out of bed, moved the wallet from under the mattress and placed it underneath the carpet. After another minute or so he decided that *that* hiding place wasn't good enough, so he got out of bed and found *another* hiding place, this time in a cupboard next to his bed that contained a china chamber pot. He dropped the wallet into the pot and got back into bed.

After a short while, he decided again to find a safer spot, so he proceeded to take the wallet out, only to discover that the pot had been used by the previous guest and had not been emptied. No wonder Phyllis was collapsing with laughter. She laughed even more when I gallantly retrieved the wallet and took it to the bathroom to wash. I had to hang the notes on the radiator to dry.

The last time I told that story was to friends and relations at my property in Australia. I had flown out the entire family (twelve of us) for an Oz Xmas, and once more Anthony had to listen to the tale of the wallet. Anthony, who never misses a chance to make a pun, murmured for my ears only, 'I remember it well. I was really pissed off.'

Anthony is now a grown man, of course, and married to Celia, who keeps him smiling. They have two daughters, Tallulah and Lily, and Ashley, who is the youngest. They are all a credit to him, being extremely clever (they make me feel an idiot) and having obtained university places, and have already travelled the world in their gap years.

But back to Jersey . . . I was booked for a one-week engagement and was very well received. Jersey had been invaded by the German army and occupied for almost the entire period of the war, so when the war was over and won, the Jerseyites were ready to celebrate and be entertained. The food was great too – although still rationed, there was abundant fresh fish, lobsters and mussels from their coastal waters and delicious potatoes and tomatoes. Coming from London, where food rationing was more severe, we really enjoyed the Jersey hospitality.

It was about this time that I first became interested in the game of golf. With a small set of clubs I had bought at a pawnshop I would make my way to St Brelade's Bay and, with hardly a soul about, I would try hitting the balls with my driver along the deserted beach – deserted except for an overturned rowing boat some 150 yards away. I used the rowing boat as my target. Then I moved in closer with my seven iron and tried pitching a shot to the boat area.

As I walked towards the boat to retrieve my golf balls I saw it move! This was odd as it was fifty yards from the water's edge. When I was almost there the boat turned over and revealed a young couple who had been doing 'what comes naturally', under the shelter of the boat. I apologised to them and asked if my golf shots hitting the boat had worried them. 'Too bloody right they did,' said the young lad. 'I thought the bloody Germans were back again.'

*

Of the several trips I have made entertaining on the *QE2*, one voyage from Honolulu to New Zealand holds a memory I particularly cherish. I shared the cabaret spot with Victor Borge, not an easy man to get to know. I tried on several occasions to get him chatting but found him very distant. Although a very funny man on stage, Victor was almost devoid of humour whenever our paths crossed. He was in his eighties then and may have been ailing. Whatever, after a couple of tries, I gave up and just nodded as we passed on deck or in the restaurant.

After we left Hawaii we were buffeted by the trade winds. For 24 hours or more the ship was tossed like a cork on the water. There was no sign of life on board – passengers took to their cabins, and bingo games were cancelled as were dancing lessons. Very few bothered about meals as *mal de mer* affected every one of us, including the crew.

Next day, when sailing was back to normal, Victor sat down for a drink with me and my wife. Knowing a comedian is always ready to listen to a topical joke, and knowing I couldn't use it, I offered the joke to Victor.

I said, 'Victor, you say to the audience: is it true that yesterday when we went through the date line we lost a day? When they answer yes, you say: why the hell couldn't we have lost yesterday?'

His reaction told me that he could do without my joke contributions – all I got was a short snort from him. I wished I hadn't bothered.

That same night I was in his audience. What a superb comedian he was – great timing and with dexterity at the piano that amazed as well as entertained. I was quite thrilled and surprised when he went into my suggested joke: 'Is it true that when we crossed the dateline we lost 24 hours? Why the hell couldn't we have lost yesterday!' Rapturous laughter and applause – so much so that it actually threw him. He could hardly find his way back into the comedy routine he had been doing for many years.

The next day I was sitting at the same table as the day before. Victor made his way over and said, 'Hey, Bygraves, got any more jokes like the dateline one?'

Victor passed on a short while after, and so went one of the best laughter-makers I have ever known.

FAX FROM MAX

For the past few years I have spent the English winters in Australia. I love England but I would rather be in the sunshine! There is plenty of work around entertaining Australian audiences and over the years I have built up an enviable following. There is little to compare with an Aussie audience enjoying themselves and I am always ready to perform for them.

While in Australia I write for our local Bournemouth paper – the *Daily Echo*. 'The Max Fax', as my pieces are called, helps to keep me in touch with my friends in Bournemouth, and saves me writing long letters. The readers seem to like what I write about – life in Australia or the stars I have met at Attunga Park, the name of the property where I stay in northern New South Wales.

Apart from family and relatives, there is a constant stream of fellow artistes who call in on their way to their next engagement, and it is always good to see them. I've welcomed Rolf Harris, Shirley Bassey, Ronnie Corbett, Frank Ifield, Val Doonican and The Krankies, plus quite a few others.

Here are some of those faxes that have appeared – for me they are as good as keeping a diary.

The MAX FAX

Max Bygraves writes to the *Daily ECHO* from Australia

Brits abroad make Sydney shows sell out

AT THE moment I am in Sydney for four concerts. Today I have the day off so it was down to the harbour on to the ferry to spend a glorious day at Manly.

On the way I seemed to meet more Brits than I meet in Bournemouth. I was most flattered to be stopped every few yards by people recognising me saying hello – most unusual.

I then discovered the QE2 was docked for three days down at Circular Quay, the crew and the tourists were making the most of being ashore. You'd have thought you were in Southampton.

Like a true theatrical I told them that tomorrow I am appearing for two shows at the Sydney Town Hall, right in the centre of the city.

When I returned to the hotel this evening there was a call to phone the manager at the Town Hall. I did, and he was bubbling over because we were getting bookings galore from the QE2 and were fully booked at the 1,500-seater for both shows.

"Fancy having to travel 11,000 miles to see you," remarked one punter from Macclesfield.

I have worked the cabaret on the QE2 in most parts of the world so I usually know the captain and crew fairly well, the maitre d' of the Queen's restaurant is Colin who looks after my wife, Blossom, and me whenever we are abroad, really well.

You may have read that Colin and several others among the crew of the QE2 purchased a racehorse last time I was abroad.

The news is that the eight owners have more than trebled their investment in prize money, so that the crew quarters constantly sounds like the offices of William Hill – long may their luck continue.

Once, in the 1960s, I was conned into taking a quarter-share in a racehorse with my manager.

It cost us more than £5,000 each when it was discovered the trainer that owned the racehorse had sold a quarter-share of the same horse to nine other mugs, so I have kept well away from the Sport of Kings since!

More next week.

Max Bygraves writes to the *Daily ECHO* from Australia

Cruellest cut of all was at Coolongatta

COOLONGATTA is a holiday resort on the borders of New South Wales and Queensland. When I first came in the early '70s it was a town of mostly double-storey buildings with corrugated roofs. Today the transformation is astounding.

We – my wife Blossom and self – are in one of the many high-rise blocks that dominate the skyline. Alongside are cranes preparing the next block, reminding me of what Bob Hope once said of London: "There are so many cranes, the fog comes in shredded."

In future, if anybody asks me what I remember most about Coolongatta, I'll tell them: "I had the worst haircut I've ever had in my life." This happened today.

I took an early morning stroll along the beach then headed back through the town. I spied a men's hairdressing saloon that was empty (I should have guessed why).

This suited me. I bid the barber "G'day", then took my seat while Dave finished reading the runners and riders page.

Dave was tall, military looking, I guessed about middle aged. "How would you like it?" he enquired. I told him to shorten it around the ears and to make the top a tiny bit shorter. Dave nodded his head in a knowing way (I hadn't noticed he was wearing a hearing aid).

He produced a large pair of electric clippers, similar to those that sheep shearers use. He was a rare breed of hairdresser – he had no conversation. With the first fall of hair on my black plastic cover-up, I should have got up and left but I'd left it too late. Dave was in his own world, he was obviously thinking of the first race at Southport, Queensland.

I watched my hair come away in chunks, enough to have stuffed a cushion. I don't know if you can remember those pictures of Elvis Presley getting his first army haircut when he was called up. Dave brushed me down. I stood and looked in the mirror . . . I almost cried. I had never seen such a transformation.

"Is that all right?" Dave enquired. "Could I have it a little longer, please?" I asked. He wasn't in our world. He first said: "Six dollars". In British currency that's about £2.50 – to a good hairdresser that's what I usually tip. "Six dollars?" I asked in surprise. "You've got the senior citizen rate," Dave told me with just the flicker of a smile.

When I walked into the apartment and removed my hat the first joke of many came from Blossom. "There's been an air raid." I asked her if it looked bad. "Not if you intend going into a monastery," she giggled helplessly.

They say a bad haircut is only bad for a month, so I will be counting the days until I get back to my regular man in Westbourne to enquire if he repairs haircuts. Maybe Blossom will quit jokes like "Home on leave?" when I walk into the room.

The MAX FAX

Max Bygraves writes to the *Daily ECHO* from Australia

Fond thoughts of the girl from Tiger Bay

THERE are few journalists writing about a celebrity who can resist a dig at their subject. This is because most writers sincerely believe that readers prefer the sordid rather than being "too nice". Not only that, it's much harder being nice than disparaging – the copy comes easier.

At present I am writing my fifth book – to be called Stars In My Eyes – for release in October next. It's a simple format: how I met them, how I found them, how they impressed me. This idea has given me a great deal of pleasure, but what I have promised myself is that I must not be unkind or bitchy – even though many of my subjects have their dark side there seems no point in disclosing this.

I have dozens of friends past and present I have written about, including names like Danny Kaye, Alfred Hitchcock, Bud Flanagan, Judy Garland and almost 50 others.

In a week I will be appearing at the Twin Towns Theatre where a few years ago I saw an old friend, Shirley Bassey,

performing. This evening, under a blood-red sunset, my favourite time for writing, I put the following piece down to be included in the book. Here is an excerpt.

She (Shirley Bassey) has survived in a business that is twice as hard for a female, she has scored because of "know-how"; lots of people are talented but Shirley has that awareness, keeping her on top, year in, year out. Never overdoing television appearances, and, like Sinatra, she will introduce a new song only if it suits her delivery. The rest of the time she gives the audience what they have come to hear . . .

She will stun them with the latest frock that gets oohs and aahs from the females in the audience; when the audience gives the obligatory standing ovation she will gather up the bouquets, wipe a tear from her smiling eyes and never overdo the encores – a consummate artist, a survivor.

We shared the same agency for several years and trod the same boards at different venues in the UK. We have been friends for 30 years or more, but my most memorable evening was a night in Australia when she was "on the wagon", but succumbed to a glass of champagne – "Just the one".

Two hours later on our sixth bottle of Dom Perignon she confessed to me the struggle this girl from Tiger Bay in South Wales had to get where she belongs.

The drives up the A6 to dates up north for one night stands – the tough audiences she had to win over as a teenager, the trying to make the drive in time to get the electric iron plugged in to press a dress that had been crumpled in a suitcase because there was no place in the two-seater to hang it. Then to rehearse with a band "that couldn't tell A flat from a bull's foot". Not for just one night but for dozens of nights – week in, week out. If she wanted to pay the rent there was no alternative.

On this night she laughed about it all, but you can see why so much has registered in her performance – nobody does it better.

Max Bygraves
writes to the *Daily ECHO*
from Australia

Rain at last
Down Under

A REALLY happy day in this part of
Australia today, the reason is RAIN –
glorious rain – there hasn't been any for
more than six weeks.

Though we have two 35,000 gallon
tanks in the garden, we've had to restrict
ourselves – no running taps, a mugful of
water for teeth cleaning and showers that
are switched off after soaping then used
sparingly for washing off, but today that
beautiful liquid came in a deluge – it's the
reason for so many happy faces.

I once wrote a song for a movie titled
"Gotta have rain". The opening lines
were:

> *If you didn't have rain*
> *Then you couldn't have flowers*
> *You couldn't have flowers*

> *If you didn't have showers*
> *Nowhere to swim – no babbling brook*
> *There'd be no fish to catch*
> *On the end of a hook.*

The BBC included the song clip in a
TV show I did last Christmas Day. Since
then, letters have poured in asking for
copies of the music, which I don't have,
but I know there is much interest in this
song because I get requests for the words
from teachers all over the world. Not only
that, there is annually a royalty cheque
which I send to a wildlife charity.

So if you happen to get some flooding
in the UK like last year or a fire in a
nearby forest give a thought to those
Aussies that have no homes because of
bush fires.

It has made it a bad season too for
tennis fans. The Australian Open has had
farewells from some of the world's best,
mostly through accidents. Their No. 1 in
the world, L Hewitt, was knocked out last
night.

Agassi had to leave with a dodgy wrist.
Venus Williams and Mary Pearce have
had to pull out, which leaves only one real
star – Pete Sampras – "and he's no
chicken", which was the comment of an
Australian commentator (Sampras is 27).

All in all, as much as I love
Bournemouth I'd rather be here enjoying
the work, the audiences, the sun, the
fabulous seafood, the fresh tender steaks
and the milk that I drink lots of because
it's so good.

Before I make you too envious, there is
too much graffiti, too many bad road
accidents, far too many murders, so as
they say on Crimewatch, "sleep well and
be happy".

The MAX FAX

Max Bygraves writes to the *Daily ECHO* from Australia

Celebration for sex-mad Francie was sober affair

A FEW nights ago I was invited by Clive, the manager of a large wine store, to his house for a party. He didn't say what it was in aid of but told me I'd get a pleasant surprise.

He seemed a decent chap, so I accepted the invitation.

"Hello," he said when I knocked at the door. "What are you doing here?"

"You invited me last week and told me not to be late," I said.

"Did I?" he asked, blinking away the sleep.

"Look, it's obviously a mistake. We'll be on our way." We turned to leave.

"No, don't go," he pleaded. "Come in for a drink." Then, raising his voice: "Look, Edna, look who's arrived – Mr and Mrs Hargreaves."

Edna said: "I know what's gone wrong – it's the *dog*'s birthday. It was Clive's idea to have a party but he's a bit forgetful."

Edna informed us that their "love" was five years old that very day. "Well, if I had a drink I'd drink his health," I said jokingly.

"What will it be?" I told him a beer would do and probably a lemonade for Blossom.

He pondered. "Beer? That's awkward."

"Don't worry – gin and tonic would be fine."

"Ah that's awkward too, got tonic – no gin."

I thought how strange for the manager of a large wine and beer store not to have two of the most popular Australian drinks.

I suggested a glass of white wine. But then he confessed he and his wife were non-drinkers.

This from the man who had advised me on the different vintage reds, malt whiskies and best port in Australia.

I told him to forget it and how sorry we were for interrupting his evening. He comforted me and told me to say "Hello" to the dog before I left.

Clive went to an outside kennel and returned with the largest bull terrier I have seen.

"This is Francie," he said removing his lead. Francie charged at me on the settee and began doing obscene exercises on my leg, his mouth frothing.

Edna helped Clive to get him off my leg. "Come and see us again," they shouted as they bundled him back to the kennel.

Later Bloss asked me: "Did you enjoy that?"

I told her: "No – but I think Francie did."

Max Bygraves writes to the *Daily ECHO* from Australia

Ruffling the feathers of the Kiwis

THERE is a friendly rivalry between Australia and New Zealand.

I say friendly but it can become unfriendly, especially on the cricket pitch or in the boxing ring. The jokes about each other are more barbed than the Brit/Irish back in the UK – and funnier.

If you haven't been to New Zealand it can take a good couple of days by sea from Sydney, in some of the roughest seas encountered.

The media is never shy to stick a few sly lines in to antagonise. The latest is in today's Sydney Morning Herald and it's going to ruffle a few feathers.

As you probably know, New Zealanders are referred to as Kiwis, and the kiwi bird is the mascot of New Zealand.

A genetic study published today has proof that the bird is more closely related to Australia's emu than New Zealand's flightless bird, the extinct moa.

Now you would think a responsible daily newspaper wouldn't have the gall to go back 68 million years to report on some dotty scientist digging up fossils, then have the DNA tested so that an announcement could be made to start a war between the two fairly unexcitable peoples.

Think of the strain it will put on the Kiwis – what will they do with all those rugby shirts for instance?

My visits to New Zealand are many. The one incident I remember most is one glorious day when I met an old friend in Auckland. I hadn't heard from him for many years and his name was Ronnie Ronalde. We broke the box-office records when we both topped the bill at Great Yarmouth for a season back in the 1950s.

We had lunch by the harbour and, with our wives, found lots to talk about. Ronnie is a good bloke and when the meal was over I asked him if he did any work these days. He told me he gets the occasional request to whistle If I Was a Blackbird, and recently he was the subject of the New Zealand version of This is your Life.

When we got outside the restaurant the storm clouds had gathered. I made one or two attempts to get a taxi but we weren't quick enough. After 20 minutes or so I saw a taxi emptying its passengers about 30 yards away, and being with one of the world's greatest whistlers I called to Ronnie: "An empty cab! Whistle it quick." He didn't and we lost the cab.

"Why didn't you whistle Ronnie?" I asked. "Because if I had done I would have lost my teeth – top and bottom," he replied.

The MAX FAX

Max Bygraves writes to the *Daily ECHO* from Australia

THERE are many people who have seen me at different venues around the world who write me complimentary (and non-complimentary) letters reminding me that they saw me in a show in London or Blackpool or Brighton.

Today I received a lovely card from a lady now living out here in Sydney, New South Wales.

Her name is Emily Rogers and on May 9 she will celebrate her 90th birthday. Emily worked alongside my mother at Guys Hospital, south London, and would dearly love to hear from me. Her son, Roy, has asked me if I will pop into the party to give her a big surprise.

I replied by fax to tell him that I had to be back in England for a concert at Southend on May 9 so it would be impossible, but to tell her to have a great party and to raise a glass to my dear old mother, Lily Bygraves.

The mention of my mother's name coupled with Guys Hospital brings back vividly an incident that makes me smile at the memory.

It was 1940 and Mum was being kept busy by the bombing of London by the German Luftwaffe. Stretcher cases plus the walking wounded needed the attention of the entire Guys staff.

My elder brother Harry, myself and my younger sister Lily had all joined the forces – my younger sisters had been evacuated and Dad had been sent to Liverpool to unload ships.

Six children had suddenly disappeared from our small two-roomed flat in Bermondsey. She was used to preparing breakfast for eight hungry people, now it was just breakfast for one. I was safe at an RAF camp at Weston-super-Mare, Harry was somewhere in Wiltshire and Lily was enjoying being a mother's care. Poor Mum had to sleep alone in a shelter at night. Mum had bombs dropping around her almost every night of the week.

Guys Hospital had been partly closed and Mum had taken a job at a factory to pay the rent. What I noticed when I came home for seven days' leave was that Mum was always happy – always singing and always generous. I could hear her before she got to the door, singing There'll be Blue Birds Over etc.

She was a pretty flaxen-haired blue-eyed smiler and I guessed that she had stopped at the pub for a "top-up". But no. I eventually found out that she was working at Gordon's Gin as a packer and sampling some of the produce.

At first I was angry until I realised that poor old Mum was trying to forget the loss of her family. We all returned safe and well. It was hard for us to imagine that the person who suffered most in that war was Lily Bygraves, all alone and afraid. I sometimes want to kick myself for not being more understanding and I did my utmost to make the rest of her life happy, as did my brothers and sisters.

It is why on May 9 I will remember to raise a glass to Mum's friend, Emily Rogers. Cheers.

The MAX FAX

Max Bygraves writes to the *Daily ECHO* from Australia

Unbeatable innings from a gentleman

BORN in 1908, cricketer Sir Donald Bradman, who died this week aged 92, had a career most professionals say will never be beaten or equalled.

He was Australia's greatest sportsman and television programmes paid him the sort of homage reserved for royalty and residents.

Young people in this country have showered him with accolades.

They know of his batting averages, his contribution to sport and the love of his country.

He survived the "Body line" bowling and later in retirement the stories about match fixing distressed him.

He guarded his privacy, and the Australian public and the media respected that. He wasn't keen to be idolised, but he was the only man to knock up 6,996 runs in test cricket.

The gentleman who thought the most honest and noble way of life was to play the game. If not, well, it just wasn't cricket.

In the days before stadiums were filled by the rock and rollers Don Bradman could fill the Oval and Lords to capacity.

My father once took me as a 12-year-old to see the great man on the off-chance that we may be able to purchase a ticket or two to see Bradman in action.

It was reckoned there were as many people outside as there were in. For two hours we sat outside the Oval listening to the applause and trying to put our minds to what was happening.

There were no transistor radios at the time, but now and again word would pass around that "Bradman hit a four, Bradman hit a six . . ." We could almost count the score by the roar of the crowd.

The only picture I can remember of him was a cigarette card given away with Players Medium. I had two sets: I completed the first after asking uncles and aunts (who later died with lung cancer) for their cigarette cards. I bought the second set complete and framed at an antique market in Bournemouth a couple of years ago, for £18.

One of Sir Don Bradman's comments was: "It's been a wonderful innings."

The MAX FAX

Max Bygraves writes to the *Daily ECHO* from Australia

Germans are baring it all in the Aussie newspapers

ONE of the joys of reading Australian newspapers is the coverage given to world news and affairs. The journalists seem to be far more humorous in their reporting which seems to take out much of the tragedy that world leaders seem so good at stirring.

Sometimes a report makes you want to re-read it, because it seems incredible, like an item that appeared in today's Sydney Morning Herald, but I know for a fact it can be true. This piece of reporting came from Germany – I wanna tell you a story . . .

During the 1980s I was asked to fly to Berlin to open a fete presented by the British Army of Occupation. The wives of serving personnel provided jams, pickles, home-make cakes etc, very much the same as an English fete held in the church hall except that this was put on in a

stadium where Jesse Owens, the American athlete, won a gold medal, and where Adolf Hitler refused a salute for this black record holder.

The British Army did a superb job of entertaining my wife and me by taking us to most of the sights that to tourists are a "must see" – Spandau, the home of Rudolf Hess since the end of the Second World War, the Berlin Wall, Checkpoint Charlie. We crammed so much into the next 24 hours after doing the honours at the fete.

Our last visit was to a park where we were invited by the captain to stretch our legs. Just before the WAC corporal came to a stop, my wife Blossom said: "I think I just saw a naked man."

She had gone no more than 10 yards when walking towards us in deep conversation were not one but two gentlemen with not a stitch on.

They stepped aside to let some children on bicycles go past, then carried on chatting while the captain and the corporal WAC tried to pretend everything was normal.

Suddenly the park seemed to be full of men and women, starkers, and this brings me to the story in today's Sydney Morning Herald, with the headline: "Germans unveil a passion for undressing". The picture they printed would probably be a little raunchy for our sedate town served by the Daily Echo.

It seems the Germans are hell-bent on walking about in all weathers in the altogether. At the height of the Christmas shopping three Father Christmases were caught on camera in the town of Frieburg.

There is an organisation of NA (German Nudist Association) "that aims to take free body culture out of its shadowy existence", according to its president, Wolfgang Weinreich.

But I mean, three Father Christmases in one day! When my wife read the article all she could say was: "I hope they had long beards".

The MAX FAX

Max Bygraves writes to the _Daily ECHO_ from Australia

Manipulated by the media show

I AM reluctant to join in with the argument on whether television programmes teach or corrupt our thinking.

Until last night I hadn't given it much thought, but in the company of several people, after dinner at a rather splendid residence on the Gold Coast here in Australia, I must say that much of my thinking has changed.

Half a dozen of us had a discussion. Apart from myself they were people of the world and knew how to put their thoughts into solid argument.

For instance, they noted that we, the viewers, are manipulated in such a way that we, poor devils, hardly notice. Take sport on TV – and there is so much of it here in Australia at this time of year. It's only when you think about things you realise how that old box in the corner can change our attitudes without us noticing.

Who gets the most time on the screen, the good sport who gets on with the game or the player who keeps questioning the line judges, argues with the umpires or breaks a racquet or two?

The answer is obvious but the point our little discussion was making was the sport had gone out of sport.

This attitude applies to most of the media too. There is an old saying that was attributed to Fleet Street that goes "never spoil a good story by telling the truth". So we will be fed this for the rest of our lives probably.

In tennis one gets a little longer to study the personality of the player. I watched a game a few days ago where the commentator tut-tutted at some of the behaviour. You could almost hear him shaking his head in disbelief at the leniency of the umpire. It wasn't until the credits rolled I saw the name of the commentator – John McEnroe!

The MAX FAX

Max Bygraves writes to the *Daily ECHO* from Australia

Eight days afloat on the good ship Saga Rose

TODAY we said goodbye to the Saga Rose, a trim-shaped cruise ship that left Southampton last January bound for a round-the-world cruise.

We boarded the Sydney eight days ago to travel up the beautiful Barrier Reef. The Saga Rose is now halfway on its journey, and I joined the delightful crew and genteel passengers for my cabaret shows.

In all the years I have made such trips, this one stands out. The captain, a proud Welshman named David Warden-Owen, has the crew and staff organised into a smoothly-running team of workers who happily see that the passengers are comfortable. Their clockwork direction is almost unnoticeable – as they say at sea, "everything ship-shape".

Today we are at Darwin, 2,000 miles from where we boarded, almost outside the Sydney Opera House. We will fly back in four hours, the journey up took eight days.

Our guide through the Reef pointed out the island where Captain Cook pulled in for repairs to his damaged ship, the Endeavour.

It took three months to make it seaworthy again.

Your mind is blown by the hardships these navigators faced.

They endured storms, hurricanes and becalmed seas and they made it back to England by sail.

We were treated to lectures, one by the actress Susannah Leigh, who unfolded secrets of her time in Hollywood with a most interesting insight to her co-star Elvis Presley.

Another most interesting lecture was by Sir David Nicholas, once a reporter with ITN, who rose to be chairman of that most honourable news team. His delightful wife, Juliet, had many a yarn to tell so that coffee at elevenses was filled with mind-boggling stories, not only about news-gathering but with untold stories of the U-boats in the Second World War. Did you know that more lives were lost in the Caribbean than at Pearl Harbour? More than 5,000 – twice as many as Pearl Harbour. Riveting stuff.

Standing by a stretched limousine at the end of the gangplank was our driver Barry, waiting to take us to the airport. I asked him to take us through the city as it was 15 years since I was last in Darwin; then it was being rebuilt after the typhoon that destroyed the entire town and killed many back in the early 1970s.

We passed the Entertainment Centre where I had appeared all that time ago. When I pointed it out to the 26-year-old driver, he said: "Strewth, you must be older than God!"

Max Bygraves writes to the _Daily ECHO_ from Australia

Revival of the old melodies

THERE seems to be a turn-around in popular music. Looking at the charts which number the best-selling records, way out in front is Robbie Williams, with two albums high in the top 10.

I am convinced that the secret of his large sales is the use of an orchestra, songs written by the world's greatest tunesmiths, Cole Porter, Irving Berlin and contemporaries that gave us tunes we were able to sing, words we appreciate.

Come on, popular music has deteriorated since names like Ambrose, Geraldo, Joe Loss and the big band bosses filled the air waves with the 32-bar chimes, choruses that told a story that came easy.

I revived it to a certain extent with my "Singalonga Max" period and although it gave me a lot of financial pleasure and made several million record buyers happy, it was a passing phase soon replaced by what is referred to as "garage music".

Now and again a couple of kids get into their garage and put down a top line that is professionally worked on and becomes a hit for the record company.

Last week, the promoter of my current tour told me he was presenting 16-year-old girl twins on my programme, my heart sank when he told me they had been voted a top act in Australia.

I thought: "My God, here we go again. A pair of screamers going for notes they can't make, words the audience can't hear and a sound system so full of echo to hide their out-of-tune voices, that it'll make a mature audience take to the toilets."

But, they were a riot. Know why? They delivered songs like Begin the Beguine, Hey Mamb, Jealousy and some memorable offerings made popular by Dean Martin.

It is a long time since I heard such an ovation. I was most flattered when they approached me after the show to ask my permission to include one of my compositions (You Need Hands) in their act at a later date.

It's too soon to rejoice but we may be on the road to recovery.

Max Bygraves writes to the *Daily ECHO* from Australia

Cooking up a controversy

TODAY a very amusing but rebellious article in the Sydney Morning Herald by writer Phil Scott. He berates the TV companies for purchasing old programmes from the BBC on cooking.

He tells the Australians they are a pushover for this "cheap" form of entertainment. He writes: "It all started with Two Fat Ladies . . . those two waddling, squealing sides of beef who were both disgusting and disturbing."

Mr Scott goes on: "Then along came Jamie Oliver, cheeky undernourished Jamie. If you met his type you'd tell the wife to get back in the car and keep your hands on your wallet . . ."

He continues: "And then there's Nigella Lawson. She bites, she whips cream using only her nipples . . . it takes you back to the ''60s and those Carry On movies, when Barbara Windsor's bra flew off."

Oh dear, he castigates the British for having the affrontery to foist their "know-how" to the world when the rest of the world knows we are rated world-wide as the world's worst cooks.

"But," he adds. "The Australians do the right thing, they buy their books."

There must be something irking Mr Scott. He is the first rebel I have come across to have a go at these cheap programmes that flood the air. He doesn't mention that if you don't like it – switch off.

Personally, I have yet to meet anybody in my travels who has cooked up a recipe by Jamie or Nigella..

Max Bygraves writes to the *Daily ECHO* from Australia

Getting snippy in the terminal

MY instructions for the flight to Singapore were to be at Heathrow three hours before take-off, which we were.

The scrutiny in this day and age of hijackings and war was unbelievable, a pair of nail scissors plus a nail file were confiscated never to be seen again. The nail file and scissors were from a set that were a present more than 25 years ago. Alright, I know I have had good value but they were from a present my eldest daughter gave me.

The plane was going to be an hour late as we were to fly around the troubled Afghanistan area, so we took a walk around the shops at Terminal Four Heathrow. There were plenty of lethal weapons on sale, even though we had been searched and had to have plastic knives at a sandwich bar.

The Quantas flight reached Singapore. The exit by Aussies trying to make connections to Sydney, Adelaide and Perth etc. reminded me of last Saturday's rugby match at Twickenham.

The day before, I had completed five televisions shows for the Christmas period and I was zonked.

My wife begged me to get my head down and relax but sleep wouldn't come, even though I was comfortable in the Hyatt Hotel – one of the finest in the world – I kept thinking of my lost nail scissors. And wouldn't you just know, lifting our luggage off the carousel, I tore a nail badly on my forefinger!

The MAX FAX

Max Bygraves writes to the *Daily ECHO* from Australia

Finding spark of humour in stormy skies

TWO nights ago we had a storm. We have storms in Bournemouth, but compared to the ones in New South Wales the storms in Dorset are just a breeze. I can put my hand on my heart and say I was terrified a couple of nights ago.

Nothing Hollywood has given us in the past could be so memorable. The rain came down like billiard cues, the forked lightning came in from the Pacific lasting several seconds, followed by claps of thunder that I haven't heard the likes of in all my years of living.

Today the sun is shining, the air is calm and we are back to the 80 degrees we know and love, but the aftermath, the damage is hard to describe. We are left without electricity, which is no big deal, but a nearby town known as Dubao, almost the size of Westbourne, has suffered 75,000,000 dollars-worth of chaos.

To restore our own power I found the number of an electrician in the local yellow pages and left a recorded message for him to get in touch. A couple of hours later in answer to our call came a voice from outside the house: "Anybody home?"

I walked outside to find a tall thinking character, 40-ish, with an Adolf Hitler moustache, trying to find life in the residence.

"Daryl – electrician," he said.

Hoping to get off to a friendly start I said "Good day Daryl – my father was an electrician – I was his first shock!" His expression didn't change.

"Did you check your trip?" he asked, meaning the consumer unit.

I told him I was not acquainted with the domestic part of the house, his expression remained blank.

"Should always check the trip," said Daryl. We searched the house to try and find the control panel and sure enough the trip had tripped. "If you'd checked the trip first you woulda saved me a 10-mile trip," he said. This remark brought a smile to his lips, the play on the word trip was the key to his humour.

I saw him to the door where he almost fell over the doormat. "Have a good trip," I said.

The MAX FAX

Max Bygraves writes to the *Daily ECHO* from Australia

The scrapes I got into with my pal Sykes

ERIC Sykes and I have been pen pals for more than 40 years. When I walk down to the mail box each morning I secretly hope there is a letter from him – if there is it not only makes my day, it makes the week.

His letters are always so full of effortless humour, I savour every line. A few days ago I received an airmail I am still chuckling over. The letter was headed: "Same address, but the roof leaks".

Eric then goes on to unload the pitfalls he has encountered during the past couple of weeks, eg he stepped out of his London office for a breath of air, his hearing is not good and neither is his eyesight. An American lady tourist came up and asked him the way to Marble Arch. He took great care with the directions "go straight, follow your nose for about half-a-mile then you'll see it on your right-hand side". It wasn't until he was back inside that he realised he'd pointed her the wrong way – she was heading towards Shepherds Bush.

Not terribly funny, but in Eric's hands it is joyous to read.

We met many years ago on a show for the BBC called Educating Archie. Eric was a writer. In two short years the show had become the nation's favourite, winning almost every award mostly due to Eric's fertile imagination.

He had a good cast from the mostly unknowns that were to become household names – Tony Hancock, Julie Andrews, Beryl Reid, Hattie Jacques apart from Peter Brough and Archie Andrews. We got so involved in the clever situations we adored performing his scripts.

We didn't usually see the scripts until early Sunday mornings, then at 2pm we did them "live". At one time it was reckoned the listening audience at home and overseas, with repeats, amounted to more than 25,000,000. Twenty five million people listening to us talking to a block of wood.

Down the road from where I am sitting now is a golf course. Eric and I were playing a game together one Saturday morning. When we were finished we walked back to my hire car. Putting the clubs away in the boot I noticed I had a flat tyre.

We were both appearing at different theatres which were on the other side of Sydney Harbour Bridge, we both had matinees, this wasn't tyre-changing time.

The groundsmen was just leaving. The only solution he could offer was to sit on some sacks filled with fertiliser as his cabin held only two people. The other seat was full of his tools.

All the way along the road to the city people were looking in disbelief at these two well-known faces huddled up in the back.

We stopped at the toll gate for the groundsman to pay his toll. "What have you got there Barry?" said the tollkeeper. Barry replied: "Four bags of fertiliser and two comedians." Eric shook his head remarking: "You'd have thought he'd make us top of the bill!"

The MAX FAX

Max Bygraves writes to the *Daily ECHO* from Australia

Trust me to meet the one in 17 million

AFTER appearing on a morning radio show, I made my way along the Sydney Harbour quayside towards the cruise ship Saga Rose to join my wife who had already embarked for a nine-day trip to Darwin after sailing through the Barrier Reef.

About 500 yards from the ship I could see the bald, orange-clad figure of a Hare Krishna ready to pounce. Using an old ploy that usually deters people, I greeted him with a few words of Spanish that I know: "Buenos dias, senor!" He returned my smile with "Buenos dias, senor!" He then joined me on the quay, keeping up with my long steps, and rabbiting away in Spanish.

Australia has a population of 17 million and I had probably picked the only Spanish-speaking Hare Krishna. As we walked he was assembling his literature for a donation from me.

I am not a good liar so I stopped and levelled with Krishna's disciple. "Me – oh, English," I said. He looked and I could see what was going through his brain . . . "This bloke has just spoken to me in Spanish, slap bang in the middle of Australia, now he says he is English . . ." You could see the confusion in his dark rolling eyes.

His eyes narrow. "Where in England?" he enquires. I told him. "Bournemouth?" He now begins to tell me in perfect English of the many times he has stood outside the Arcade waiting for customers to leave Dingles and how they were all so generous.

It was a hard sell I knew I had lost. I asked: "How much?" With the same childish innocence he asked, "How much can you afford?" I gave him a $20 note which is about £8 something, hoping to get $10 change, but already he was chiming his finger cymbals, like a musical cash register, as he made his way up the quayside looking for further donations.

When I got to my cabin I tossed the book on to the bed, then went for a swim and a shower. When I returned, my wife Blossom was seated in the armchair, deeply involved in the Hare Krishna book.

"Where did you get the book?" she enquired.

"From a chap on the quay."

"It's very good – have you read it?"

I told her no, I had only got it a few minutes before boarding. She then told me she would like to get a copy of it for a friend in Queensland who would enjoy reading the book. I told her she could have my copy – I'd get another one.

The MAX FAX

Max Bygraves writes to the _Daily ECHO_ from Australia

Writer's block takes place of writer's cramp

FOR a couple of quid I am learning to work a computer.

I have three computers – one in Oz, one in Bournemouth and the other at my office in London and I don't know one end from the other of any of them. I go to this place that has a dozen or more machines with students seated studiously picking up "web sites" – avoiding "glitches" and surfing the "superhighway".

For me it is a new adventure; my wife, too, has decided to enter this weird world and we trade thoughts from these digital marvels that relay from outer space – we are only 10 feet apart but it doesn't matter, we still keep dialling for HELP.

I have had to get serious about this as I have started to write a book and after 3,000 words in longhand I have writer's cramp and am not so enthusiastic about it.

Stars in my Eyes is the title of a book about celebrities I knew. The publisher is looking for 20,000 words and I fear I am not going to make it.

When I started the book I jotted down the names of people I met, liked, stayed friends with – and there were almost a hundred about whom I felt I could share some memorable moments with the reader.

The first half dozen were easy, then it got harder. Although I had worked side by side with Tony Hancock and shared dozens of meals and drinks with him, when I put pen to paper I found I hardly knew him – the same with Judy Garland. After writing she was a joy to work with, which I did for a couple of years, there was little else to tell.

Oh yes, I could go to a library and read some hack's assessment but I wouldn't like it to be that sort of book, so I will just type out this little message: D!*x4-117!'BCX-.

STARGAZERS A TO Z

There are many kinds of stars in the show business world – bright stars, fallen stars, lesser stars, has-been stars, almost stars, shooting stars, tomorrow's stars, comeback stars, current stars and the megastars who will be remembered for many a long day!

I have had the privilege and pleasure of knowing many of these stars well; with others I have had only a nodding acquaintance. The following A to Z of some of the many stars I have met, may be of interest.

EAMONN ANDREWS

During his lifetime, Eamonn Andrews did it all – he boxed, he commentated confidently and he sang – but what I remember is his affability. Begin talking to Eamonn for the first time and you'd think you had known him all your life. I have seen versions of *This is your life*, the television classic devised by American Ralph Edwards, in many different countries, but none compare with the show handled for many years by Eamonn.

I was caught for the 'Red Book' and told 'Max Bygraves, this is your life' when I was on stage at the Prince of Wales

Theatre in London. Eamonn and I remained friends from that meeting in 1961 until the day he passed on. We golfed together, met at charity events, had quiet drinks in cafés and told each other naughty stories – mostly Irish ones. I had countless invitations to his home outside Dublin, but sadly never made it.

During one *This is your life* programme, where the unsuspecting catch was Tommy Cooper and I was there to say nice things about him, the three of us found ourselves alone. Eamonn remarked that all the impressionists on the TV screen were doing impressions of us – Tommy was for ever being impersonated by some wit in a red fez saying, 'Just like that . . .', while I was impersonated with drooping hands, uttering 'I wanna tell you a story . . .' Eamonn, of course, was impersonated in a rich Irish brogue with ' . . . and tonight, this is your life!' We were all fodder for a laugh.

As we stood there sipping our gin and tonics, Tommy mentioned we were the three most impersonated men in Britain. There was a pause, and then Eamonn observed, 'If anything happened to us three, half the comedians on television wouldn't have an act left.'

Eamonn's passing was a big shock to me because he seemed indestructible. So did Tommy Cooper. Of this trio – Eamonn, Tommy and me – I am the only survivor. But when the end does come, I'm sure I'll hear an Irish voice and it will be Eamonn standing outside the Golden Gates, holding a red book and saying, 'Max Bygraves, tonight, this *was* your life!' And a red-fezzed conjuror will utter, 'Just like that!' If this does happen, I can use one of my own catchphrases: 'I've arrived and to prove it, I'm 'ere!' Then we'll all go for a gin and tonic.

JULIE ANDREWS

At fourteen Julie Andrews was already established on the showbiz calendar. She was a child star with her parents who made a living as Ted and Barbara Andrews, a well-known singing act. Young Julie made her name with a most pleasing voice and her diction (which was a little over the top, even for an English kid) plus a smiling presence. She was a little tall for the plaits her mama fussed over during breaks. Later on we were to star together at the London Palladium, she as Cinderella to my Buttons. Julie was still in plaits then.

Our very first meeting was at the birth of the BBC radio show *Educating Archie*. The star of the show was the ventriloquist's dummy, Archie Andrews (no relation). Julie was cast as Archie's girlfriend. During the 'song spot', she would lend her voice to a suitable ballad for a twelve-year-old (as she was playing), such as 'Christopher Robin is saying his prayers'.

At rehearsals, Julie would sit listening to us, sucking on half a Meggezone to clear her sinus. She made a good audience for the 'read-through', laughing at the funny lines provided by scriptwriter Eric Sykes. It was hard to imagine then that one day this young lady would be a world star – as Eliza Doolittle and later as Mary Poppins (a movie that rescued Twentieth Century Fox from bankruptcy after they spent so much on *Cleopatra*, a box-office disaster starring Elizabeth Taylor and Richard Burton). Harder still to imagine was that this very, very proper English lady would one day bare her breasts for the world to view in *Victor/Victoria*, a movie directed by her husband Blake Edwards. But that's show business.

If I was asked to remember one particular moment spent with Julie, it would be an evening Christmas concert performed for Her Majesty and staff at Windsor Castle. As we walked through the hallowed halls we passed a figure in full armour – visor, leggings and battle axe. It was awe-inspiring. The last thing you would expect is a comparison to a cigarette-lighter, but Julie murmured, 'We have a Ronson like that.'

ARTHUR ASKEY

'Big-hearted Arthur', they called him, and the story goes that Arthur never found out why. The reason, I am assured, was because at the top of his fame, and as one of the profession's big earners, Arthur Askey never got round to buying anybody a drink at the canteen bar.

I was told that Richard Murdoch, his co-star, coined the phrase after Arthur once wandered into the bar – last, so as not to buy a round – and said to the barmaid: ' . . . and one for big-hearted Arthur.' Somebody wrote a song on the theme:

Big-hearted Arthur they call me,
Big-hearted Arthur that's me
I'm clean, if not very clever . . . etc.

What amazed his fellow thespians was that this well-loved broadcaster didn't see the cynical side. He actually believed it was a term of endearment.

I got to know Arthur rather well over thirty years and always found him great company, full of energy and with unashamed cheek at helping himself to any of your best jokes. I had a fun routine about taking a cinema usherette out on a date: I told the audience that during the interval the same usherette would sell ice-cream from a tray looped round her neck. I got a big laugh when I told them that because the ice-cream was so cold the sellers were equipped with electrically heated bras (laugh). I finished, *'You* are surprised – *I* was shocked!'

When Arthur heard me deliver the usherette routine, at a show in Bournemouth, he came backstage to my dressing room and asked me: 'Are you terribly fond of that electrically heated bra joke?' I told him I was, but in his own way he cajoled me into 'sharing' the joke with him.

On a *Sunday Night at the London Palladium* TV show, I did the joke. Next day an indignant Arthur phoned me and reprimanded me for cracking 'our' joke on television. 'Everybody now will think I stole it from you.' 'I'll give you another one you can use,' I told him. I rattled off a couple of good one-liners that I thought would suit his style, but he didn't reckon they were as good as *our* 'shock' joke.

He came to my house on several occasions and was taken by the décor. 'Who did it?' he asked. I told him it was my wife Blossom. Then he asked who did some of the paintings on the wall. Again, I told him it was Blossom. In the garden, he said, 'I suppose this is Blossom's work too?' I nodded. At that moment, my wife appeared with tea and sandwiches, apologising for the thickness of the bread. She confessed to Arthur she had never learned to cut slices of bread from a loaf. 'Thank Christ there's something you can't do,' he laughed. Blossom dines out on that one.

One of the saddest moments I can recall was my visit to St Thomas's Hospital just across Westminster Bridge. Arthur was in a private ward there, and when I entered he was being helped by a nurse to hop to the bathroom. He had recently had an amputation and lost the lower part of a leg. Just before I arrived he had been told that the second leg had to come off. Arthur's legs were his main prop – those silly little jigs he did made the jokes that much funnier. 'What a bloody way to end a career,' he said, almost to himself. There was a long silence. I could think of nothing to say. Eventually Arthur broke the silence: 'I must phone my agent and tell him no more Long John Silver parts.'

Shortly after, Arthur died, not so much from the two amputations, more from a broken heart.

Even as I write these lines tears well up in my eyes, more in admiration for this top performer than anything else. I feel privileged to have had him as a mate.

ROWAN ATKINSON
I met Rowan Atkinson as I was descending the stairs at the Palladium. 'Hello. How are you?' I asked.

His mouth formed an 'O' and his eyes grew wild, like a stag caught in a car's headlights, but there was no reply. I never found out how he was.

HYLDA BAKER

Hylda Baker was a contradiction, a tiny woman with an astute brain. Apart from 'Good evening' and sometimes 'Goodnight', we rarely had more than a couple of words together, even though our dressing rooms were next door to each other.

We were booked for the show *Latin Quarter* in Blackpool. It was a box-office smash. Hylda was a supporting act and did very well. She had a white-faced stooge who stood a few feet away, and hardly ever moved from the spot, while Hylda poured out her private life to the audience. Sometimes a glimmer of recognition appeared on the face of the stooge. Hylda would get a big laugh then with a line that was to become a national catchphrase, 'She knows, y' know!'

It surprised many people who watched her act that she could not make friends easily. To help her overcome this, she purchased a miniature live monkey. When I would pass her dressing room, I'd hear her talking. I thought she was having a go at her agent, but in fact she was talking to the monkey! She was a most demanding performer. Naturally, the public and many of the profession would also talk to the monkey, which looked like one of those creatures that sits on a hurdy-gurdy while the owner turns the handle and collects the money.

Hylda found the monkey a wonderful conversation-opener. But the other artistes in the show – me included – began to hate the bloody sight of it. Its screaming and 'pong' didn't endear Hylda to any of us.

When the show folded, we went our separate ways. Suddenly, television discovered Hylda Baker. She had a long run, then fizzled out. In the meantime, the rumour went about that she was a difficult customer, and as the public lost interest she became even more so.

I was most surprised to see her in a restaurant with Leslie Grade, brother of the agent Lord Grade. Leslie had his arm around her shoulder, more like lovers than agent and client.

When they said their goodbyes, Leslie pecked Hylda on the cheek and then he made his way to my table. He sat down with a resigned shrug. I remarked that he seemed 'awfully nice' to somebody who was reckoned to be 'difficult'. Leslie's reply was: 'Always be nice to artistes who have seen better days – they have a funny way of making comebacks.'

How true those words were – it was only a few months more before Hylda hit the big time again, and bigger than ever. Somebody had seen her potential and scripted a series where Hylda inherits a pickle factory. Partnered with Jimmy Jewel, who had also been resurrected, they proved to be a smash hit. Hylda Baker had more impersonators than Edward Heath and Tommy Cooper.

I don't really know what happened after that. I can't recall her funeral or who attended – I could have been overseas – but what I do recall is a very lonely lady who made it to the top with very little help from others. She even had a number-one record, when she teamed up with actor Arthur Mullard to duet a song from the musical *Grease*.

No doubt had she lived today she might have been making records with Robbie Williams!

RONNIE BARKER

One of the best ideas Bill Cotton Jnr ever had when he was Controller of Programmes at the BBC was the pairing of the *Two Ronnies*, Ronnie Corbett and Ronnie Barker. Bill realised that winning duos like Morecambe and Wise, who had defected to ITV, could offer more scope than stand-up comedy. A double act can come up with ideas that the single comedian finds difficult. Bill had tried it a couple of times with some lesser-knowns, but it hadn't had the right chemistry. With Barker and Corbett, the format worked a treat, and went on for many years.

It seemed strange that at the top of their popularity they called it a day. Ronnie Corbett decided to carry on entertaining in a solo capacity, but Ronnie Barker opened an antique shop somewhere near Bishop's Stortford.

Ronnie Barker and I had spent quite a lot of time corresponding with each other, Ronnie always writing to me on notepaper headed 'HM Prison Slade' (as in *Porridge*). His letters were always cheerful. In one letter I wrote to him, I asked whether he was interested in a Shakespeare manuscript, in his own typing. Or if not, did he want a Queen Anne bicycle in going order? That was the sort of banter we both enjoyed. His replies are treasured among my souvenirs.

His delight at getting my name wrong – as Mr Hargreaves – makes me proud. I got to know and adore Ronnie Barker, a one off.

SHIRLEY BASSEY

Shirley Bassey has survived in a business that is twice as hard for women. Lots of people are talented, but Shirley has the 'know how' that keeps her on top. She never overdoes television appearances and, like Sinatra, only introduces a new song if it suits her delivery. The rest of the time she gives the audience what they come to hear: 'Hey, Big Spender!', 'Something', 'Kiss Me Honey, Honey Kiss Me' and a dozen more standards.

She will stun them with her latest frock, getting oohs and aaahs from the women in the audience. And when she receives the obligatory standing ovation, she gathers up the bouquets, wipes a tear from her smiling eyes and walks offstage – never overdoing the encores. She is a consummate artiste, and a survivor.

We shared the same agency for several years and trod the same boards at venues all over the UK. We have been friends for thirty years or more, but my most memorable evening with her was in Australia when she was 'on the wagon'. She succumbed to a glass of champagne – 'Just the one'. Two hours later, on our sixth bottle of Dom Perignon, she confessed to me the struggle that she – a girl from Tiger

Bay in South Wales – had made to get where she is today, and belongs.

The drives up and down the A6 to one-night stands 'up north'. Hurrying to arrive in time to get the electric iron plugged in so she could press her crumpled dress. Then to rehearse with a band that, more often than not, ' . . . couldn't tell A flat from a bull's foot!' And to win over tough audiences when she was still a teenager. This went on for dozens of nights, week in and week out. If she wanted to pay the rent and become known, there was no alternative.

On this night she laughed about it all, but you can see why there is so much emotion in her performances. Nobody does it better.

MICHAEL BENTINE

Mike Bentine entered the world of show business principally to be a writer of comedy material. This was many years before he took part as one of the Goons – that came later.

When we met, which was shortly after the end of the Second World War, he had teamed up with an old RAF friend of mine named Tony Sherwood. Tony was a pianist but had a great desire to try comedy. I don't know how the two met, but they were working hard on an act, calling themselves Sherwood and Forest.

They were doing very well at it too. I had heard them on the BBC programme *Variety Band Box*, Tony as a tolerant Englishman feeding Mike's Mad Russian, an accent he could perform convincingly. Alas, there wasn't a huge interest in this type of twosome and soon the act split up. They went their separate ways, Tony to work as a club pianist and Mike still trying to put an act together that was commercial, staying way out on the fringe.

Notice was taken of Mike when he found props in a blown-up motor tyre and the back of a chair, which he made into a convincing number of things such as prison bars, a large key and a chopper to visually illustrate his spoken routine. We met occasionally on variety bills at theatres in the provinces. We also finished up with equal billing at the London Palladium.

I cannot think of Mike without recalling an incident at the Nottingham Empire in 1950. I had just received a telegram from the 'czar' of British show business, Val Parnell: 'Congratulations. You have been chosen to entertain Their Majesties King George VI and Queen Elizabeth at the London Palladium'. I was filled with trepidation.

Also on the bill in Nottingham was a comedian (I won't mention who) who came up with a suggestion that made me even more frightened. At supper in the digs we were all boarding at that week this comedian said, 'The reason you have been given a Command Performance is because Val Parnell is aiming to "make or break" you.' There was a silence as we sat there letting these words sink in. Then Mike said, 'Why the f..k would Val Parnell try to "break" him? He's trying to *make* him. Val needs star performers and [pointing at me] this bloke's got it. If you don't believe it, compare our applause at the end of our acts and then listen to *his*. He's got it!'

This was the confidence and belief I needed at that moment, and I was grateful to Mike for spelling it out. When I got on the stage in front of Their Majesties, it was probably the turning point in the career I have now enjoyed for more than fifty years.

Michael Bentine was a founder member of the *Goon Show*, but left to pursue a career that helped to support his lovely wife and family. He was a loving father, a really 'hands on' fellow, who nursed quite a lot of tragedy in later life. He was never envious of others' success, always a friend, and a great entertainer. He has to be among 'my very favourite people'.

THE BEVERLEY SISTERS

The three Beverley Sisters are charming, dedicated interesting ladies whom I have known and adored for more than fifty years. In July 2002, we had the great pleasure of appearing together once again, on this occasion for Her Majesty's 'Jubilee Walk-about' among the adoring public at Lewisham. The 'Bevs' – chic, perky and looking half their age – had the public applauding their singing and laughing at their banter as if it were yesterday. Joy, who was once married to the famous footballer Billy Wright, together with twins Babs and Teddy, were all dressed identically, and were the photographers' delight. When opening the daily paper the next day, I wasn't surprised to see they had space a politician would kill for.

It was a great pleasure to be able to introduce them to Her Majesty and Prince Philip, who enjoyed the chat we had. I told Her Majesty I had been in the 1950 Royal Variety Show, the last show her father had enjoyed before his untimely passing, and then two years later was selected again with the fabulous Beverley Sisters.

As the Bevs talked, you'd have thought they were conversing with their next-door neighbours instead of Royalty. Once they get going, it's hard to stop them – they could talk the hind legs off the proverbial donkey. I once kidded them it was like listening to stereophonic, but on this day it seemed more like *quadrophonic* (they had a daughter along)! But the Queen and the Prince enjoyed the chat. There must have been more than 20,000 out on the streets of Lewisham to wave Union Jacks and blow kisses to our Royals. And didn't they love it. The Queen suddenly seems thirty years younger when she basks in the adoration.

Back in our dressing rooms at the Broadway Theatre we went over the day. I managed to get the Bevs' interest in a joke I was going to do on my appearance later. It went like this:

'The car in front of me had the number plate ER 1. It stopped and this well-dressed lady got out. She ran up to my car, opened the door and kissed me. It wasn't Her Majestey in ER 1. It was Esther Rantzen!'

That joke got the biggest laugh of the night.

CILLA BLACK

Although Cilla Black and I have worked in studios and venues together, we have actually met only once, and that was in Australia. I knew her husband Bobby quite well, but Cilla and I come from different generations. The time we met was at a concert one Sunday evening, a charity to help one of variety's 'greats', Jimmy James, who was having a bad time through illness.

During the afternoon rehearsal, The Beatles then manager, Brian Epstein, sidled up to me in the Stalls and told me that he was handling a young woman singer from Liverpool. She had never appeared in London's West End, so the Prince of Wales Theatre must have seemed daunting to her. He asked my opinion on whether he should allow her one song or two.

I suggested if she was good the audience would be the judges. Let her rehearse two numbers. If the applause warranted it she could do the second. I don't know why I was handing out advice to this gentleman, who was also handling one of the world's greatest money-makers, The Beatles, but he was keen to have my opinion.

On the night, with a packed audience, I was in the dressing room getting ready for my stint and so missed Cilla's spot. In the car on the way home my wife, who had seen the concert all through, remarked that she had enjoyed the new girl singer from Liverpool. I asked how many songs she had sung, and the reply was 'three'!

GEORGE BURNS

I knew George Burns when he was a much younger man – he was only 76! I'll never forget our first meeting. It was at the Dorchester hotel. He had given me his room and floor number. I went straight up and knocked at the door. A small, frail, bald-headed man dressed in a burgundy silk dressing gown opened the door.

'Is Mr George Burns here?' I enquired.

'Just a minute,' said the little old man, and went back into the room.

The same little old man emerged about twenty seconds later, this time wearing a silver toupé and thick glasses and smoking a nine-inch cigar. 'What can I do for you?' asked George Burns.

The transformation was astounding. I just stood there laughing.

'What are you laughing at? Have you never met a leprechaun?'

That was exactly what he looked like. So many people must have said so that he decided to get it in first. We became friends from that day on. He told me so many 'stories' – it was hard to sort out the truth from the fantasy. But there was never a silent minute with George.

He would talk of Al Jolson: ' . . . not a great guy as a friend but a superb entertainer, unasahamed schmaltz.' He'd tell of Fanny Brice, Sophie Tucker, Sam Goldwyn, Ronald Colman and many many more, all first-hand stories. I was content just to sit and listen. The talk went on for more than two weeks – at rehearsal, at dinner, in the limousine. What's more, he never repeated himself.

Many of his 'stories' had macabre pay-offs, like the following (think of George telling it between puffs on his Havana corona . . .):

'You think of fans that adored people like Sinatra and Johnny Ray? The equivalent in our day was George M Cohan, the great American songwriter and entertainer. He would give five shows a day and the crowd for the next show would be lined up round the block, waiting to get in.

'Between shows Mr Cohan and the supporting cast would take refreshments in the Green Room, then get ready for the next performance. It was a great honour to be on the same bill as George M Cohan. He played all the best dates, the auditorium was always a sell-out and your date book was filled for many months.

'At the beginning of a tour that opened in Philadelphia, two hoofers [male dancers] joined the show. They had not been in the business long and were wide-eyed at being on the very same programme as the great George M Cohan. One afternoon, between shows in the Green Room, one of the dancers plucked up the courage to talk to George M, who was in deep thought at the end of the bar. He said, "Mr Cohan, this is the greatest thrill of our lives. We are new to show business and to be an opening act on the George M Cohan tour is beyond belief! It would give us so much pleasure if we could buy you a drink."

'George M explained that he had just received some bad news – he had lost his mother and would prefer to be alone. To which the youngest dancer replied, "We know how you feel. Two weeks ago we lost our suitcases!"'

ALMA COGAN

If the Reaper hadn't called at an early date for Alma Cogan, she would have still been a big star today. I feel sure of that. She had the energy, the charm and the talent to have survived in this tough male-dominated business, in the same way as stalwarts like Vera Lynn and Sophie Tucker have done.

With the giggle in her voice and twinkle in her eye, plus a dress sense that made the fashion trade take notice of what she was wearing, she was always news. It's a great shame that Alma was taken from us at such a very young age.

If I had to come up with one special memory of Alma, it would be the night she came to see *Do-Re-Mi*, the show I was appearing in at the Prince of Wales Theatre. She was escorted by songwriter Norman Newell. After visiting backstage she suggested we go to eat at a small place she liked, just off Piccadilly. We had a wonderful meal and chatted happily. I had recently written a song called 'You need hands', which was having a good time on the hit parade. Talk of this led us to the reading of palms, which Alma was interested in and had become a bit of an expert about. After reading my palm and Norman's, telling us both that we were the most complicated twosome she had come across, she went on to describe the life lines, the success lines, when we would have illness and so on.

I asked if I could look at her palm. She extended her hand across the table, and I was surprised to see on her lily white mitt just three lines, none of the cracks and crevices that filled Norman's and my palms. I traced her life line, which was short and rather faint. 'Is this your life line?' I asked. She answered that it was, and then giggled, 'I won't be around much longer.' From a lady in the prime of her life, in her mid-thirties, such a ridiculous statement made us laugh.

I forget where I was when the news came over the radio that Alma was no more. She had failed to beat the cancer that finished her, and British show business suffered a great loss.

JIMMY EDWARDS

Jimmy Edwards was the first comedian I ever heard use a four-letter word on stage. This is pretty harmless by today's standards, but back then . . . my God!

As Jimmy blew a scale on his euphonium, he'd get redder in the face. The audience would join in the progression up the scale – 'doh, ray, me, fah, soh, lah, tee . . .' Jimmy would make the supreme effort to hit the last 'doh'. A long chord followed and then came the congratulatory applause as Jim wiped his brow. He would then tell the audience: 'When I made that last note it would have been impossible to wedge a tram ticket between the cheeks of my arse.' Sure it was risqué, but how heartily they laughed.

When he was told by one manager to take the four-letter word out of his act, Jimmy substituted 'bum' for arse. But it was never the shock laugh he got with the original.

DAME EDITH EVANS

I am not always convinced that the eccentrics known in the

theatrical world are truly eccentric, or whether they play a part some time in their careers and enjoy it so much they change themselves into that image.

The first time I met Dame Edith Evans was at a small rehearsal room in Soho. Director Billy Chappel had this wild idea that she and I should do the duet 'I Remember It Well' from the musical *Gigi*, which Maurice Chevalier and Hermione Gingold did so well in the movie version. When Billy Chappel suggested this I was doubtful – I was still in my thirties while Dame Edith had passed seventy. I know there is such a thing as theatrical licence, but . . . In the event, Dame Edith and I hit it off really well and in all modesty we were the hit of the night on a star-studded bill at London's Palladium.

It was arranged that when we took our bows I would present her with a glittering evening bag. She would take it from the wrapping in front of the audience, who would then be treated to her famous exclamation: 'A handbag?' At this £100-a-seat 'do' those two words rocked the walls of the Palladium – so well done, perfectly timed. It received a standing ovation. I felt proud to be the escort of this septuagenarian as we strolled offstage to the wings.

Three years later I had my own weekly show on Thames Television. Eric Davidson, one of the writers, had been at the Palladium when I performed with Dame Edith, and he suggested we repeat the scene on television. Dame Edith was contacted, '. . . and would simply adore being with young Max!' Davidson came up with a good comedy idea: Edith would keep getting my name wrong. She would refer to me as Mr Hargreaves, Max Bywaters, Mr Bygroves, etc. It was arranged that we would send the finished script to her a few days before rehearsals began, and then knock it into shape, as most actors do, when rehearsing face-to-face.

The Rolls delivered her almost to the door and unaided she followed the floor manager into the rehearsal room, the script clenched in her fist. She didn't bother to pass the time of day – her first words, while waving the script like a suffragette, were: 'I will not do it! No way will I do it! Get rid of the writers! I will not utter a word!'

We stood there – the director, wardrobe mistress, make-up director and I – all wondering what it was she would not do. We all thought the idea of getting the name wrong was wonderful. She seated herself in the middle of us, still murmuring, 'I will not do it, not for all the money in the world.' She had really put a fright into us. I timidly said, 'What is it, Dame Edith? *What* won't you do?'

'Get your name wrong. What an insult. You have worked so hard all these years for the public to know your name. You cannot permit this sort of thing. Throw it out. There are much better ideas, I'm sure, for your talent.'

Poor Eric Davidson, who'd thought it was a good script, had skulked away to the end of the room. The Dame went on: 'You should be proud of the name. It takes a long time to get the public to learn to know our names and I will not lower myself . . .' and on and on.

We did as she bid and wrote a different entrance, with no Mr Hargreaves or Bywaters. She was happy with the alternative. When we performed 'I Remember It Well', there was an ovation similar to that night at the Palladium.

Four weeks later she invited my wife and me to see her show at the Haymarket Theatre. She was wonderful, and got a deserved standing ovation from the international audience. The manager came to our seats in the Stalls to ask if he could escort us to Dame Edith's dressing room. When we arrived the room was filled with well-wishers and friends of this talented and friendly person.

When she saw me she hushed everybody quiet, saying, 'I want you to meet one of my very favourite men.' The Dame took my arm and told the small crowd: 'Here he is, the one and only MAX HARGREAVES!' And she meant it. I learned later from her lady companion that she had been rehearsing my name for a week. She had memorised a two-hour show, but could not remember Bygraves. I wonder what would have happened had I been Arnold Schwarzenegger!

FAMILY ALL STARS

My family consists of my wife Blossom, whose taste, forsight and understanding have helped to keep us all together, and the 'immediates' – my son Anthony and my daughters Christine and Maxine.

Anthony is my right arm. He has his own family – his lovely wife Celia and our three grandchildren – but he still devotes much of his time to helping others, especially me. His 'know how' and expertise has kept me working and enjoying these twilight years, making them a joy.

My daughter Christine, now living with husband Barry in Australia, does the same job when I am spending time there, which I seem to be doing more and more these days.

My youngest daughter Maxine is the mother of two fine boys – Oscar, who recently got into Oxford, and Barnaby, now fifteen. Barnaby looks like he could become a top golfer. He not only beats me, he plays seriously with the pro at his course. Maxine's marriage was not a success and for some years now she has had to bring up these two boys on her own in a different country (Spain). She is an expert at floristry and works hard at being a mother, father, adviser and organiser. Hardly a day goes by when Blossom is not on the phone to Spain, talking to Maxine with love and guidance. I know this is so – I've got the telephone bills to prove it.

GOLDIE

One Sunday, I was asked to play in a Pro-Am tournament at Leatherhead Golf Club. There were many well-known personalities playing. It suited me because my house was near the course, so there was no travelling to be done. All I needed was my studded shoes, which I took to the locker room to change into. I was appearing at the Palladium at the time and on the previous night, I had had a mishap.

I made my entrance on a horse, a big wonderful creature named Goldie. He was a circus horse, trained by Vera Cody. By touching him in different places and giving him different words of command, he would perform. When I dismounted, I would bring him to the front of the stage and ask him questions; then by tickling him in the right spot and rewarding him with a few lumps of sugar, he would appear to the audience to be talking back to me. Actually, what happened was an offstage microphone was used, with a man faking a voice for Goldie. After the chat, I would mount him again, and the band would play a 'Tea for Two Cha-Cha'. Goldie would swing his bottom in time to the music – and exit to tumultuous applause.

The night before the golf tournament, Goldie had trodden on my toe. As I wore soft shoes the pain was excruciating. What's more, he didn't move once he was on my foot – unless you've had a ton of horsemeat on your toes, you won't appreciate how painful it can be. Now it was the morning after. I was in the locker room inspecting my bruised toes, when one of the players walked up behind me and said, 'Hello, old boy, how are you?'

Without looking up, I said, 'Not so good – I've got a bad toe. I'm just wondering if I can get round eighteen holes.' He snorted and said, 'Bloody sorry about that, old chap', then he walked off, clanking as he went. I looked back – I still shudder with embarrassment each time I think of it – and saw that the man I had been complaining to was Douglas Bader, the legless pilot, hero of the Second World War, the man who had known more pain with his lost legs than any man living. Yet here I was beefing about a couple of bruised toes! I made a vow never to complain about my lot again. I don't know whether I have stuck to it, but I meant to.

TONY HANCOCK

Tony Hancock was one of radio's laughter-makers in the sixties and seventies. We fed off each other well with Eric Sykes's scripts. I still have a letter that Tony wrote to me a few days before he took his life at the hotel overlooking the harbour in Sydney. In the letter he wrote: 'I will always appreciate the time you advised me to slow down my entrance at the Palladium . . .'

Tony had asked me to come to his first night at the Palladium. By then he was a star name but nonetheless he was a worried man. The thought of following some of the 'greats' who had appeared on that hallowed stage made him puff his cigarette three times as fast.

On the big night Tony entered from the wings at breakneck speed, eager to get to the microphone and into his act. He was wearing a tuxedo!

When he asked me after the show if I could suggest anything he could put right, the first thing I suggested was to get rid of that well-tailored tuxedo. It wasn't his image. Either get an ill-fitting suit or wear an astrakahn-collared jacket. Also, I said he should enter slowly, stopping halfway to the mike to look back into wings as if disgusted with some enemy offstage. As the welcoming applause subsided, he should look offstage again and then murmur to himself (so the audience could hear), 'Flippin' stage managers!'

He told me that those changes made all the difference. It's no wonder – every comic strives to get a laugh with the first words he utters.

The reason Tony and I got on so well was that he was fascinated by my war experiences. Being a year or two older than he was, and having served in the RAF for four years, did give me more knowledge, but I think everybody of our age group was well aware of Hitler's whereabouts for those years. Most of London still bore the scars of Adolf's onslaught – the bomb craters and skeletons of buildings were testimony to all the havoc Adolf had wreaked. Tony often asked me to relate stories to some of our drinking pals, such as Hattie Jacques, Eric Sykes and producer Roy Spear.

Tony particularly liked me to tell the story about a bombed-out Londoner I met early one morning after a bad night's bombing.

I was home on leave and had had to take cover in an air-raid shelter. When I got dressed and back into uniform – the only clothes I had – I walked out of the shelter into the bright morning sun. After the sound of ack-ack guns and exploding bombs all through the night, things were eerily quiet. I made my way down the pot-holed street and came across a middle-aged man in his trousers with shirt hanging out, sitting on a pile of rubble that had once been his house. Seeing me in RAF uniform, he said, 'Why weren't you up there last night?' I told him I didn't work on Sundays, which brought a smile. He then said, 'When this lot's over, I'll never buy another bleedin' German sausage!'

For some reason that was one of Tony's favourites.

Only yesterday afternoon there was a re-run of one of the *Hancock's Half Hour* programmes on the radio. So funny. What a performance. What a pity.

ROLF HARRIS

Australia Day is a serious event for Australians. The armed forces parade in towns and villages to pay respect to those who gave their lives not only at Gallipoli but in recent wars like Korea, Suez, Vietnam and the Falklands.

This is the year 2002, but my mind goes back to an Australia Day five years ago. Walking up the road towards our house were two men, one I recognised as Ken Jekyll from our Sydney agency. The other looked like a vagrant tagging along. The bearded, unkempt person with paint-spattered trousers I eventually recognised as Rolf Harris.

Rolf works hard at being eccentric, but he is good company and really is a lover of nature. Later on he told Blossom the names of the trees, plants and flowers on our property. I stood there listening, feeling about as useful as an ashtray on a motorbike!

He kept plying us with advice: 'Don't let the cattle near that noxious weed. It's poisonous.' And: 'Those jacaranda trees need more space.' One of the cattle raised its tail to do its business. Rolf in ecstasy said, 'Ah, lovely. That goes onto the land, the finest fertiliser you can have.'

Blossom rustled up some lunch with a bottle of wine, and the four of us chatted about England, which seemed like the other side of the world – which it is. Rolf is a genuine sincere bloke, full of anecdotes and a pleasure to listen to. We had a stuffed signature bear by the door, which we ask visitors to sign – there are some famous names who have put their signatures on our bear. Rolf added a cartoon of himself, with the caption: 'Couldn't bear to leave.'

When Ken and Rolf made their way to their car, Blossom said, 'What a wonderful man.' Rolf's been a pal ever since. I still tell him a joke I sometimes pull on Aussie audiences: 'The British government's idea for my visits is that they'll keep sending me to Australia until you take Rolf Harris back!'

BENNY HILL

If you were to ask me who the most famous comedian in the world was throughout the seventies, it would have to be Benny Hill. The last time we were together he told me that his Thames Television shows were being shown in 28 countries. It's probably more now.

Not only the most famous but possibly the richest funny man around then, his fame was unbelievable. Once when I was working on a QE2 cruise we were just leaving Rio de Janeiro. A young honeymoon couple, hearing my English voice, asked if I had ever heard of Benny Hill. I boastfully told them I knew him. They gazed at me as if I was the Messiah, and followed me around the ship for almost a week.

On the same trip we made a stop at Tristan da Cunha in the South Atlantic – population 187, all Spanish-speaking.

A woman who had been evacuated to England when the volcano was threatening to erupt, passed me a note to see if it was possible to get a signed picture of Benny when I got back to the UK. I gave the note to him on my return and he was more surprised than I was that somebody from somewhere so remote should know of his work.

As I said, he was very wealthy, but he didn't bother too much with money. His greatest stimulant came from his work – to make a gag or funny routine come to life was really all he cared about. The press tried on several occasions to make copy from his spartan way of life, but I don't think Benny ever bothered to buy a newspaper. I don't think he knew or cared about monetary rewards.

This story isn't all about Benny. It also concerns a friend of mine named Johnny Kelly. Johnny is now retired and lives in Bognor down in Sussex. At one time he owned the Hillingdon Social Club just a few miles from central London. This was in the late forties, just after the war, when many people were in the mood to be entertained. Johnny kept me going with regular bookings at the club where I always did extremely well with the audience – he paid me £3 a show.

There was one particular day in late summer when I couldn't make a date because of a full week's engagement in Jersey. I wrote to Johnny to say how sorry I was, but recommended a pal I had met who was free and would appear for £2.50 (two pounds ten shillings in those days). I told Johnny his name was Benny Hill, and I said in the letter: 'I promise he won't let you down.'

Johnny still carries that note around. It is held together with Sellotape now, but he will produce it any time the occasion demands. Not too long ago I was appearing in Bognor and Johnny came to say hello. Sure enough, the note came out. Johnny gazed at it in disbelief, shook his balding head and murmured, 'Imagine, Benny Hill for fifty bob!' 'Did you book him?' I asked. 'No fear. He was too bloody expensive!'

Both Benny and Johnny Kelly have passed on since then, but their laughing faces and valued friendship remain treasured memories.

LENA HORNE

The American soul singer Lena Horne came to the attention of the British public as the result of some close-ups in early Hollywood jazz films. Lena was put in those films mostly to add a little glamour. She just oozed sex and mystery – easily the most glamorous gel around in the fifties.

At that time my name was usually quite prominent on most billboards, as they call them in the US (placards in London). But I found myself at the Birmingham Hippodrome 'second top' to the fast-rising Lena Horne. We were there for a full week, two shows a night.

A couple of years before this I had done a season in the pantomime *Cinderella* at the Theatre Royal Birmingham, and so had got myself quite a following from the theatre-going public. It wasn't a mass following like the rock groups enjoy today, but I had quite a few devoted fans. Of course they booked tickets for the variety bill I was performing on with Lena Horne.

She was (and still is) lovely – flashing eyes, a smile that lit up her so interesting face, a gorgeous figure, everything about her was beautiful, and so photogenic. It seemed we were in for a happy week, with good business and a crowd I knew I could score with.

I don't know who planned the running order of the show, but I was on in the second half of the programme – the dancers opened, then it was me, followed by Lena and the orchestra, conducted by MGM musical director Lennie Heyden. I didn't know it at the time, but he had quietly married Lena before their arrival in England.

Well, on the Monday night, it went very well, so much so that the music for my exit had to keep going. While the orchestra was still playing, the resident conductor handed

STARS IN MY EYES ☆

the baton to Lennie, who was then supposed to start Lena's entrance music. But – and I am not proud of this particular moment – my fans led the audience to carry on with the applause. Lennie Heyden didn't know what to do. The audience were calling 'More!' and Lennie, who had spent most of his days with sophisticated audiences, was all at sea. I don't think he had ever encountered a provincial crowd wanting a performer to do encores.

The stage manager told me to go out and take another bow. I shouldn't have done so, but I did. Poor Lennie stood there bemused, with folded arms. Lena was in the wings wondering what to do. This was her first appearance in Britain. At last the crowd settled down, and the show carried on. The orchestra played some wonderful arrangements by Lennie and Lena was appreciated the way a top-line star deserves to be.

I met them both many times after, when Lena was 'tearing 'em up' in cabaret. I'd go to her suite and, in mock dismay, Lena would back away with her arms held high, saying, 'Go away, Max Bygraves – go back to Birmingham!' Then I'd get a sweet kiss on the cheek, those eyes would flash and she'd smile that smile. Love you, Lena.

NOSMO KING

Mr Nosmo King was a gentleman in the real sense of the word: he was a 'gentle man'. We first met when he was in his fifties. To somebody like me, in their twenties, he was 'old'. My parents were about the same age. In those days, fifty *was* old age.

The fifties were not the 'good old days' that many still remember as the best years of their lives. London was a mass of smoking chimney pots that polluted the air, so much so that the winter months brought thick 'fogs' referred to as 'pea-soupers'. As a young man in my first car, which was a Ford Anglia, I remember driving home in these 'pea-soupers'. If my wife was with me, she would get out of the car to dangle a white handkerchief in the nearside headlight, so that I wouldn't mount the pavement.

Poor Nosmo King, who was asthmatic, dreaded those pea-soupers as he had to fight to get his voice in shape for his performance as a monologist. He would walk on stage, puffing on the large Havana cigar that he always used as a prop, to punctuate his delivery and to give him time to build up his patter for the punch line.

Mr King, as I always called him, took his name from a NO SMOKING sign that he saw in a railway carriage going to Sheffield. He did a fair amount of broadcasting for the BBC and was a good canopy name for a touring show we were both in, entitled *For the fun of it*. Every week a different town. Mr King and his wife (naturally I called her Mrs King) always had the best dressing room. Both of them were very thoughtful to younger performers in the cast, especially the John Tiller Girls, twelve young and attractive teenagers, as well as myself and Frankie Howerd who were just entering the show-business world.

They would invite Frankie and me to their comfortable dressing room and pass on advice and 'know how'. During the show Mr King would wander to the wings and watch us, to see if we had paid heed to his good suggestions. I always knew he was there even though I couldn't see him – I knew his cough. After I had finished my stint he would wave me into the dressing room, pour me a hot cup of tea and then tell me whether I had got his advice wrong or right.

Microphones had a habit of breaking down quite frequently in those days, so the advice handed out by Mr King was about the art of projection. Audiences would soon let you know if you were inaudible. 'Speak up!' 'Stop whispering!' Another was: 'Oi! We've paid out money, don't keep it a secret!' Unless you could do something about it, you would be very embarrassed. So the advice on voice projection from Mr King was readily accepted, and has stayed with me to this day.

One morning during the tour I was at the theatre in Sunderland, walking across the stage. I had come to see if there were any letters for me. I say letters, but the only person who wrote to me in those days was a part-time agent asking for his ten per cent of the £15 a week I was earning.

On this particular day I almost bumped into Nosmo King. He was happy to see me and decided that this would be a good time to learn the art of projecting to a full house when the microphone was playing up.

He stood centre stage and asked me to look at an EXIT sign in the circle. Then he said, 'Now pretend that sign is somebody's head. Don't talk like we are talking now. Don't shout, but throw your voice at that sign.' It worked, it really worked! And it will work for anybody trying to make it on the 'greengage' (the stage).

When I read Nosmo King's obituary in *The Times*, I wrote a letter to the editor to tell of the kindness of this gentleman, and of the help he enjoyed passing on to people like me. My letter didn't appear in the paper (at least, I don't think it did – I couldn't afford to buy *The Times* too often then, so I may have missed it), so I'm glad that I now have an opportunity to express my thanks to a lovely man.

DANNY LA RUE

You would travel a long journey to find a more generous person than Danny La Rue. His gifts and kindness to people he likes are legendary. He has survived in a crowded profession on sheer talent – as a female impersonator he has no equal. And although the years are passing many of us by, he still manages to attract audiences at home and abroad – and leave 'em laughing.

If anybody was to ask me what his faults are I could only think of one: he loves to 'rabbit'. He really can talk the hind legs off the proverbial donkey. When Danny gets a touch of the verbals it is best to shut up and listen, or say, 'We must get home 'cos of the babysitter!' Let me tell you a Danny La Rue story.

My wife Blossom and I went to see his show at the Regent Theatre in Sydney, Australia. The show was great. Afterwards we were invited backstage to Danny's dressing room. When we got there we were told by his road manager Jack that Danny was on the other side of the stage talking to some members of the Sydney Ballet, and that he would not be long. Jack gave us a glass of champagne and we waited . . .

We were both hungry, having had no food since breakfast time. Sydney, like most cities, seems to close down foodwise after 11 p.m. But we waited . . .

Blossom kept glancing at her watch every two minutes. Then after almost twenty minutes of waiting she came out with a classic line that Danny still dines out on: 'We didn't have to wait this long for the real queen!'

Danny will not have to wait too long to meet our present Queen because today (15 June 2002) the newspapers announced the Birthday Honours List, including an OBE for Danny. It's well deserved.

SPIKE MILLIGAN

I knew Spike Milligan mostly through Harry Secombe, Michael Bentine, my close friend Eric Sykes, and some other comedy writers. I found him hard to get to know. If I enthused to him about one of his television broadcasts, he'd look furtively around as if to find an exit quickly, and walk out sideways like one of his Goon characters. Similarly, in the fifty years of our acquaintance, I never once heard him praise or say he liked another performer. His only acknowledgement to a startling piece of new talent would be to draw his cheeks in, suck his lips and lift one eyebrow – as if to say 'not bad'.

Spike never looked for praise. But if a critic rubbished one of his books by saying 'I didn't enjoy this book as much as the last one', Spike could dream up swear words about the critic that were so obscene, you'd wonder if they were his own invention. In short he could cry 'blue murder'.

But there is no denying he was a 'one-off', an innovator, a great creator, who became a benchmark for future funny men. He also knew his audience and how far he could go.

My favourite story about Spike was when he shared an office in Bayswater with top writers Galton and Simpson, who were writing the Tony Hancock series. There was also Johnny Speight writing the Alf Garnett hit show *'Til Death Do Us Part,* Eric Sykes writing his own top show that featured Hattie Jacques, and several other comedy authors.

With all this writing output, typists and secretaries were in demand. A new girl had joined the Associated London Scripts' team and, like the rest of the typists, was expected to make tea whenever requested – the writers spent hours sitting around the large table giving each other ideas for scripts and sipping cuppas made from leaf tea.

On one particular day, Spike returned from the loo, went into the typist's room and demanded to know who had put the tea leaves down the lavatory and not flushed them away.

The whole typing pool stopped typing and eyes went to the new girl. She timidly stood up and admitted shyly that she was the culprit. Thinking she was in for a dressing-down from Spike, she owned up: 'It was me, Mr Milligan.' Spike stared at her for a moment or two with that steely glint he was known for, then said, 'You're going to meet a tall dark stranger.'

DES O'CONNOR

I once received a letter that was memorable because of the sheer 'modesty' of the writer. I cannot remember it word for word because after I'd answered it I tore it up. I wish I had kept it, but it was usual then to receive half a dozen similar letters each week, all on the same theme: 'Can you help me get into show business?'

It was a letter from Des O'Connor. He explained that he was in the RAF, serving his conscription, but that when he was released he was going to try the entertainment business. He added that he sang a great deal better than I did, that he told better jokes and that he was much better looking. What could he do with all this God-given talent, he asked. Could I advise him how to start, and where to find an agent? And he told me to look out because when he got going he would unseat me from the perch I had and he would be the new Max Bygraves!

I took time to write him a letter with the only advice I knew how to give. It was on the lines of 'learn to walk before you run', 'get audience experience', 'gather material', 'work in pantomimes and summer shows' and 'don't be afraid to experiment'. I wished him good luck.

Several years later our paths crossed and he introduced himself to me as the writer of the cheeky letter. He had taken my advice and got a job as a redcoat at a Butlin's Holiday Camp. He thanked me. And each time we meet he tells the story to anyone who cares to listen.

I was guesting on his Thames Television show once and the story of his letter and my reply came up. Des was telling it to some writers and cameramen. I interrupted him to say, ' . . . but Des, now you are established and a well-known name, surely you must get similar letters asking how to break into showbiz, don't you?' He confessed that he did. I asked him how he answered them. He got a big laugh when he told the assembled crew: 'I write back and say, "Get in touch with Max Bygraves!"'

TED RAY

Ted Ray was a fine comedian and also a practical joker – right up to the end of his life. We had become firm friends after he had appeared in one of my television shows, where he was a big hit.

I went to visit him at the Middlesex Hospital. He was in

a bad way – a car accident had left him with a broken leg and a fractured arm, and they were grafting skin to various parts of his anatomy.

I took him smoked salmon, champagne, a cake and lots of other titbits. In no time we had the sister and nurses in for a small party. After a couple of hours Ted looked exhausted, and the sister tipped me off that it was time for Ted to rest. They all left and I was ready to say farewell. But Ted was a comedian from the old school, who learned to 'always leave on a laugh so that you'll be remembered next time you make an entrance'.

Ted thanked me for coming and then pulled himself together to tell me a final story:

'A few nights ago I needed a bedpan. It had gone midnight and I was desperate. I rang and rang the bell, but no nurse came so I attempted to do something about it myself. I lifted the bed covers off me, slid slowly to the end of the bed and managed to get to that pot with the plant in it. I took the plant out, put the pot on the floor, undid my pajamas and managed to sit on the pot. Just as I did the door opened, a light went on and there was Eamonn Andrews saying, "Ted Ray, tonight this is your life!"'

Shortly after this Ted passed on.

PETER SELLERS

I have a flat in London that looks out across the city, with spectacular views taking in Big Ben, St Paul's Cathedral and the now trendy docklands area. At varying times we have shared the block with stars like Laurence Olivier, Peter Sellers, Jimmy Edwards, Ingrid Bergman and others, but all of them moved on eventually. I think that we are among the longest remaining residents.

Peter Sellers, who lived above us, was the noisiest neighbour. When he moved in, he had the flat redesigned. For almost three months the drilling and banging drove us mad. Peter, in the meantime, was away from it all in

Hollywood. Laurence Olivier couldn't stand the noise so he moved out, checked into a hotel and sent the bill to our landlords, which they paid.

Peter had a hi-fi system installed, which had a pounding bass. It would go on throughout the night – Peter was nocturnal and played records until three or four in the morning. I had known him for more than forty years and had often called him to say hello and 'chew the fat'.

One particular night, when the music was going full blast, I picked up the phone at 1.30 a.m. and, in my best upper-class English voice, shouted at Peter: 'Now look here! If this music does not cease, I will personally have you kicked out of the building!' I slammed down the phone. The music stopped and we never heard it again.

Three days later, I met Peter in the elevator. Putting on his spiv voice he said: 'Ere, this bleedin' Lord Olivier comes on a bit strong, don't 'e? 'E phoned me the other night an' told me 'e'd 'ave me kicked aht o' the buildin'!' I looked at him, one of the game's greatest impressionists, to see if he knew it was really me who had phoned, but no! Until the day he died, he really thought it was Olivier who had given him a rollocking!

TOMMY TRINDER

He was mostly referred to as 'Trinder'. Very few of us get to being called by our surnames, but Tommy had a surname that suited him. You called him Tom or Tommy in conversation, but it was Trinder that he liked and answered to, especially when addressed by someone in authority.

Trinder had a quick ready wit and lost himself many acquaintances who took exception to this style of 'put down'. One in particular was Lord Grade. Before Lew Grade's knighthood, then later his lordship, Trinder would gently – or not too gently – describe him as the typical theatrical agent, always looking for his ten per cent. This was on the television show *Sunday Night at the*

London Palladium. Trinder got big laughs when he said something derogatory about Lew Grade. Finally Lew had had enough and asked him to stop making the Grades – Lew and his brother Leslie – the butt of his patter, which at the time was going out to eighteen million viewers.

Trinder took no notice, even when he woke one morning to find he had been replaced as compere of this top-rated show. He gave quotes to journalists who were glad to seize upon anything that had humour against the well-known 'ten-per-center'. Trinder really had a flea in his ear about him and never stopped lampooning Lew. Suddenly the good work, the work that mattered, dried up. Tommy's health failed and he finished up in a wheelchair. The delightful comedian became a bitter man, and profanity spilled from his lips most of the time.

I was invited to take part in a television show on the life of Max Miller. So was Trinder. The stage manager politely asked if I would give a hand to three others in helping Tommy to descend from the stage to the Stalls in his wheelchair.

Tommy pulled the most outrageous lines about how useless we four were, as we lifted him above our heads to place him in the Stalls as gently as possible. 'What a f. . ...g load of amateurs we've got 'ere. You'd be no f. . ...g good even as council workers!' It was typical Trinderisms and made the stagehands smile.

When we got around to paying our respects to the great Max Miller, Tommy could not hold back from berating his old adversary Lew Grade, so much so that Trinder's contribution was cut from the TV production.

There is no doubt that in his 'hey-day' Tommy was a very popular top-liner. He had the cheek of the devil. Should you ever come across any of his old recordings, listen to them and tell me why this coarse, cockney, raspy-voiced comic insisted on delivering a song in Noel Coward fashion. You would expect the Stanley Holloway sound of

'Get Me to the Church on Time', but Trinder's singing voice sounded like a student fresh from Cambridge. Whatever, he always insisted to patrons sitting in the audience, who had paid to keep him on top: 'You lucky people!' And he meant it.

MAX WALL

My first meeting with the multi-talented Max Wall was on the parade ground soon after I had joined the RAF. It was a cold winter morning in Blackpool. He was a corporal drill instructor and I was one of a bunch of rookies that he was to drill and turn into something useful for the war effort. His first words to us were, 'On the word of command, I want you all to come to 'Attention', to come together as one man. Are you ready?' We indicated that we were all set. He then eyed us and shouted, 'Attention!' We changed from the stand-easy position and obeyed – but not as 'one man'. He sniffed – in the same manner he later used as a comedy sniff – glared and growled, 'Like a bloody machine gun!'

The strange thing is that at the end of four weeks we had turned into a well-disciplined squad. At the passing-out parade, we were as good or even better than the rest. When the parade was over, to reward us, he opened a new packet of twenty Players' medium-cut cigarettes and gave out one each. We all took one even if we were not smokers.

After the war, I saw his name on quite a few variety posters at the local theatres and went to watch him on a couple of occasions. He was good, but as a performer he blew hot and cold. If the audience were not to his liking, he'd make jokes like: 'Why not all join hands and the one at the end put his finger in a light socket'. Sometimes he'd walk off to very scattered applause. He was the most unpredictable performer I ever worked with.

At Finsbury Park Empire in the late forties the orchestra leader was a gentleman named Syd Kaplan. He and Max didn't get on well and Max would direct him from the stage, much to Kaplan's annoyance. 'Give me a four-bar introduction and I'll pick you up on the North Circular Road,' Max suggested when the tempo was not right for his dance. 'I've got funny little legs.'

Later, he discovered that his medium was television. He became a 'cult' with young audiences who watched the 'box', and was in great demand. Of course, in an instant his angry face could light up with the most delightful smile and you'd warm to him.

At one Command Performance at the Palladium, he arrived late. It was raining outside, and Max walked straight into the theatre to the centre of the stage. He tapped his umbrella on the microphone and, in front of some of the world's greatest celebrities, he addressed Robert Nesbitt, the director, who was seated in the Stalls. Making no apology for his lateness, he said, 'Excuse me, is this where the concert is?' 'Get off!' shouted Nesbitt. Max put on a winning smile and replied, 'But I'm a star! Twinkle, twinkle', and fluttered his eyelashes. He wandered off into the wings where I was waiting. In his saddest Shakespearean voice, he said, 'They have no more time for thespians.'

During his spot later that evening he 'laid 'em in the aisles', which is not an easy accomplishment on a Royal Command show.

ROBBIE WILLIAMS

Sometimes I am asked: 'Who do you see coming up, to add to the stars in your eyes?' I can only think of one young performer who might be around in years to come. His name? Robbie Williams.

This fellow has talent, stage presence and savvy; he writes some good songs; and he is not afraid to experiment – all ingredients you need to keep climbing up the slippery slope they call stardom. It takes time to get it all together and he is now at the stage in his career where things can go up or down. He can either be a sincere performer, eager to please, always on time and knowing his lines – advice that the then-famous Max Miller gave to me when I was Robbie's age – or he can blow it all on the indulgences and temptations that show business makes so easily available to the successful.

If a performer hits the jackpot nowadays the financial returns are in their multimillions. International concert tours, recordings, writer's royalties, television and movies, plus a massive publicity machine and world communications, can generate fabulous earnings – so much more than was achievable by entertainers of our day.

I recently saw a Robbie Williams 'Special' from the Royal Albert Hall. It was wonderfully staged and choreographed, and Robbie commanded the stage with all the confidence of a true show business contender. Call me old-fashioned, but one thing marred the show for me and that was the unnecessary four-letter words and graphic language from the host. It seemed to jar. Maybe it gave Robbie some street 'cred' with his younger fans, but the show didn't need it.

It is how you make it, use it and handle it that dictates the outcome. I hope Robbie Williams succeeds. A performer who manages to survive in this age of 'flavour-of-the-month' pop stars, and short-lived show business careers, deserves every penny he makes.

LENA ZAVARONI

Lena Zavaroni was a child performer who blossomed at age twelve. A most likeable young lady, she exploded onto the scene when she performed on Hughie Green's *Opportunity Knocks*. She earned her laurels when the viewing public voted her 'the most likely to succeed'.

It wasn't long before she was taken under the wing of Dorothy Solomons, an agent with a string of first-class acts under contract. Dorothy spent many hours grooming this Scottish dynamo, choosing her wardrobe, having her hair styled, etc.

The first thing Solomons did was to take Lena to Las Vegas to be photographed with Frank Sinatra, Dean Martin and the rest of their clan, who at that time were 'kings' of that vast showplace. She returned with publicity that many would kill for. The BBC gave Lena a thirty-minute television programme filled with big name guest stars. It rocketed her to fame so quickly it made young Lena bewildered.

I introduced her to the Royal Command Performance audience in 1976 – I put a steeplechase-jumper's hard hat on her head to show what an uncanny likeness she had to our Princess Anne. I also guested on her TV show. There was no doubt that Lena was going to be Britain's 'Judy Garland'. She oozed the same feeling of enjoyment in what she was doing and worked hard.

Returning from a job in Australia, I was saddened to see such a dramatic change in her. She had suddenly got the idea she looked too fat – at that age it was probably puppy fat. At a benefit 'do', in the Grosvenor House hotel, she was seated next to my wife at the large table. Bloss noticed she hadn't eaten anything. Lena, who was now looking anorexic, confessed that she felt uneasy eating in the presence of others.

My wife fixed that by putting up a large menu in front of Lena so she could hide behind it and eat to her heart's content. The ploy worked that time, but of course it didn't solve her problem, and she grew thinner with each passing day. Not only that, she grew morose and distant. It was the way many at this time were going.

Lena died, and we lost one of the best new talents to appear in many a blue moon. Talent like hers is so rare it should be preserved. Sorry to finish my A to Z on such a sad note.

*

Thankfully the world is full of young enthusiastic talent, those who dream of being stars and reaching dizzy heights. Some will achieve it and some won't. This is a tough and competitive business that doesn't give too many second chances. It takes hard work and dedication – and a certain amount of being in the right place at the right time.

I've been very fortunate to have spent more than sixty successful years entertaining and enjoying my work. I have travelled the world many times, covering enough miles almost to take me to the nearest star. It's been quite a ride. I've still got my tux and band parts ready for the next booking. Maybe I'll see you there. I hope so. Until then, be like me and keep stargazing.

WOULD YOU JUBILEEVE IT?

When I arrived back in the UK just a little over a week ago, it was grey, dismal, gloomy. Heathrow looked like a dosshouse after the colourful sidewalks in Singapore and the golden sands of Australia's Gold Coast, where the jacaranda trees were in bloom and the sky was blue – those blue, blue skies you can rely on for most of the year. England seemed so downcast.

Our car ordered seven days before wasn't there at the airport, so we decided to give the driver some time as he was probably held up in traffic. We decided also on coffee and I joined the queue waiting for the solitary waitress to make coffee at the counter. There were sixteen others ahead of me. Bloss sat with the cases, keeping an eye out for our driver.

Eventually I joined her and we sat for half an hour watching the world go by. And what a dreary place it seemed. We talked about leaving these parts for retirement somewhere else, saying farewell to a government that seems to be doing its best to take away our individuality, our ambitions, our freedom. We felt like jumping on the next plane going *anywhere* and waving goodbye to England. Don't get me wrong, I love my country. I love the people and I can stand the weather. I love being English in England, not Scotland or Wales or Northern Ireland – I always write England as the country of my birth on any legal form. English and proud of it.

This frame of mind stayed with me until a few days ago. It was then the Queen's Jubilee, and slowly my mood changed. The people really did her proud. The Mall was packed, with crowds in and around the Palace – it was wonderful. Here I was looking at a different England. As Concorde flew over, the Queen and Prince Philip stood on the balcony and gloried in the affection from the well-wishers. There were so many cheers they had to reappear for a couple of encores. I know that feeling on stage when the crowd is with you.

The rockers and rollers at the concert earlier in the week showed they could put on a show that nobody else in the world could compete with – so many well-known names in show business, the estimated 200 million audience watching on television could only applaud. We were part of that audience, sitting around the TV with our family, raising glasses to our queen, who in my humble opinion shed forty years when she smiled that sunny smile. Long may she reign over us. Cheers, Ma'am.

And then yesterday, the England football team – remember that word ENGLAND – were on TV, which was another great excuse to get the drinks out. By the time this book reaches the booksellers most of this will be in the past, but today, as I write, the newspapers are full of praise for this bulldog breed that made old England's name. England 1 Argentina 0. But don't be fooled. There's a fickle public out there.

Four years ago, young Beckham retaliated after being brought down by a foul, and was sent off with a red card. Many thought he was responsible for us losing the chance of winning the World Cup. He was treated like a leper. Yesterday, though, scoring from a penalty, Beckham wiped the slate clean. Had it been possible millions of us would have kissed his feet at that moment. Even if he never put on football boots again, this likeable young fellow will be adored for quite a few more generations.

I liked a letter to the editor in today's newspaper: 'A few days ago there were millions enjoying themselves down the Mall and Trafalgar Square. There were only three arrests. Could it be the troublemakers were all away in Tokyo? ' Not so, as newspaper reports tell us that the England supporters were on their best behaviour, even though Brazil robbed us of our full glory. Could things be looking up for this fair isle of ours?'

Pass the champagne, Bloss. Cheers! Put the passports away. Here's to stars past and present that make all our lives that extra bit special and mega-kilowatts brighter. Cheers again! And God save the Queen.

[Cue Orchestra for National Anthem]
CURTAIN